calm and compassionate children

calm and compassionate children

A Handbook

SUSAN USHA DERMOND

CELESTIAL ARTS
Berkeley

Copyright © 2007 by Susan Usha Dermond
Front cover photograph © by Steve Satushek/Iconica/Getty Images

Celestial Arts and the Celestial Arts colophon are
registered trademarks of Random House, Inc.

Material from Sharing Nature with Children by Joseph Cornell
on pages 17, 44, and 48: Copyright © by Joseph Cornell.
Reprinted by permission of Dawn Publications.

Library of Congress Cataloging-in-Publication Data
Dermond, Susan Usha.
Calm and compassionate children : a handbook / Susan Usha Dermond.
p. cm.
Includes bibliographical references and index.
1. Education, Elementary—Philosophy—Handbooks, manuals, etc.
2. Self-realization—Religious aspects—Handbooks, manuals, etc.
3. Lifeskills—Study and teaching (Elementary)—Handbooks, manuals, etc.
I. Title.
LB1555.D47 2007
372.01'9—dc22
2006033155

ISBN-13: 978-1-58761-276-3 (pbk.)

Printed in the United States of America

Cover design by Toni Tajima
Text design by Katy Brown
Illustrations by Ann Miya

12 11 10 9 8 7 6 5

First Edition

I dedicate this book to all of my teachers, with
unending gratitude. Thank you.

Author's Note

THE EXPERIENCES on which I base this book come from my life as a stepparent, teacher, and school director. All of the stories and anecdotes I write about actually happened. I did, however, change the names of the "characters" in those stories unless I received their express permission, in which case I included both first and last *real* names. I thank everyone whose experiences have contributed to what I share in this book. More acknowledgments follow.

The first Living Wisdom School was founded in 1972 by Michael Nitai Deranja at Ananda Village, a rural, intentional community near Nevada City, California. Deranja is currently the director of the Living Wisdom High School and authored the book *For Goodness' Sake: Supporting Children and Teens in Discovering Life's Higher Values.* I joined the staff at Ananda's school in 1984, after six years' experience as an English teacher and school librarian in public schools. Although I had met a few wonderful teachers in my public school experience, I felt frustrated by the institutional emphasis on intellect and the dismissal of the role of feeling and intuition.

The early years of the Living Wisdom School were a grand experiment in learning how to teach the whole child, not just the intellect; in developing ways to teach children self-control rather than conformity; and in learning how to bring out the best in children—including their calm compassion. We used the trial-and-error method, with varying degrees of success! Many of those successes, as well as our mistakes, appear in these chapters. That experience was my grounding for the past ten years as director of the Living Wisdom School in Portland, Oregon.

The next generation of Living Wisdom schools has demonstrated the success of our approach and its effectiveness in urban settings. In addition to the Portland school, there are Living Wisdom schools in Palo Alto, California, and Seattle, Washington, and one is slated to open in Sacramento, California, in 2007. The core philosophy of the schools is presented in the book *Education for Life* by J. Donald Walters.

Acknowledgments

I WOULD LIKE TO THANK all the children and teens with whom I have shared the learning journey, my colleagues and friends of many years, and those who have more recently helped me with this book.

To my stepchildren who are all grown up: I am proud of you, even though I can take no credit for how wonderful you are!

Teachers are great collaborators and share their ideas generously. Thanks to Toby Moorhouse, who taught me so much about teaching children to be calm and compassionate. I work with an incredible team of teachers at the Portland Living Wisdom School: Sandi Goodwin, Helen Gorman, Trina Gardner, and Karen Busch. They have all supported this book and exemplify calm and compassionate teaching. Thank you to Jay Casbon for teaching me much about education and administration. I appreciate Carol and Bruce Malnor—both for your love of education and for your friendship. Thanks, Bruce, for all those times you said, "You should write!"

Thanks also to the Novaks, the Smallens, and the McGilloways for their support through many years. Joseph and Anandi Cornell, I so appreciate your feedback and advice. Diane Atwell and Margie Bazan, you too! Lorna Knox, my friend and colleague, never got tired of reading yet another version of every single chapter, and encouraged me when I needed it. Thank you.

This book would never have happened without those of you who supported the founding of the Portland Living Wisdom School, especially Kent and Marilyn Baughman, Michael Coombs, and John Gorman. Bob Ausbeck and Darlene and Jamey Potter, thank you for your steadfast support of the Living Wisdom School. Bent and Parvati Hansen gave unselfishly to the school and infused me with confidence. Eric and Ingrid Glazzard's love for children and education, and their passion for Education for Life, have encouraged me no end.

Many others gave so much that helped with this book. Thank you, Sue Mann, Paul Werder, Doris Blazer, the Gardner family, Laura F. Williams, David Eby, and K.L.B., for your contributions. Carla Hannaford expanded my understanding of mind-body connections and gave me enthusiastic feedback. Thank you to Thomas Lickona, for your careful reading and feedback on my book proposal, and Michael Lerner for publishing my articles. Thanks to my agent, Janet Rosen; Meghan Keeffe, my extraordinary editor at Celestial Arts; and Julie Bennett, acquiring editor at Ten Speed, who "loved the book!"

I am grateful to my sister for unreservedly supporting my writing. Thanks to Michael Nitai Deranja, who started the first Living Wisdom School and continually supported my efforts. And my gratitude to J. Donald Walters, for the suggestions on the introduction and everything else.

CONTENTS

Compassion is of little value if it remains an idea. It must become our attitude toward others, reflected in all our thoughts and actions.

—Dalai Lama, *An Open Heart*

A Matter of the Heart

WE ALL LOVE being around children who are balanced, creative, joyful. Even when active, these children are calm, not out of control. They can exert great energy to accomplish whatever they set their minds to, and they can be quiet and focused as well. They can play an active game, listen to a good story, or look for shapes in clouds for a long time. They enjoy their own imaginations and creativity. These children go through the ordinary ups and downs of childhood, but *most of the time* they are happily engaged—playing and learning with no thought of external approval or reward.

As they grow, their awareness expands beyond themselves, and they begin to understand others' realities, which in turn leads to compassion. They can willingly let a younger child have the first turn, and they cheerfully help with family or school projects. They have enough inner contentment to cope with small disappointments, and they are able to "go with the flow" of life, accepting both its ups and its downs.

As teens, calm and compassionate children are able to feel inside what is right and wrong and make choices based on their inner convictions rather than feeling pressured to go along with the crowd. They have self-control rather than being controlled by external influences.

Does this all sound too good to be true? Through my work as the director of the Living Wisdom School, a non-profit private school in Portland, Oregon, I know it is possible for children to be proactively calm and compassionate, even in a group. Let me tell you about an incident I observed.

Parents and children often visit the school as part of their school selection process. A mother was visiting with her four-year-old son, Riley, to see the kindergarten. As we chatted, the fourth and fifth graders ran out for recess and began a game of foursquare. After years of playing together they are rather good, and they have evolved a complicated set of rules for their game. Riley watched them play, obviously eager to join in. I was apprehensive at the prospect because the older children were enjoying a rather intense competition. I was ready to divert him to something else.

However, these nine- and ten-year-old boys, without any discussion, graciously let four-year-old Riley into the game. Not understanding that there was a waiting line, he intruded right into their play; they just suspended their fast pace and gently bounced balls into his square until he missed. Then they showed him how to wait in line.

It was gratifying to see the children spontaneously expand their sympathies to include a new little boy without ever being asked. Seeing his eagerness to play, they included him, putting aside their own agenda. We all know adults

calm and compassionate children

who would be reluctant to do this in the heat of athletic competition.

Although we emphasize kindness and awareness of others, no one had ever said to these children specifically, "If a visiting small child interrupts your game on the playground, be sure to stop playing and include him." What set of circumstances enabled these children to tune in to their calm, compassionate natures?

A few of these children have unusual families in which the parents live an alternative lifestyle, not in the mainstream, perhaps practicing voluntary simplicity or living in an intentional community or having a deep religious practice. However, others come from households that are more typical in lifestyle, yet their parents make very conscious decisions about parenting their children differently from the mainstream. Both groups choose our school because of its mission to encourage the development of living values, such as honesty and compassion.

As a parent or teacher you too can provide the framework for the children in your care to keep their natural spirit of wonder and joy, kindness and love as they mature and grow. As they grow into adulthood they can retain these qualities and avoid cynicism and negativity. This book will give you many suggestions for how to provide this framework—from nature activities to establishing conscious quiet time to tips on daily routines.

are your children happy, really?

As school let out one afternoon, several of the children were tearing around the playground, screaming wildly because of their anticipation of an overnight birthday party. Watching them, one of the teachers commented, "Sometimes I think that parents confuse their children's excitement with happiness."

Observe a young child inundated with too many gifts on a special occasion. The excitement of desires fulfilled will actually agitate him. He may talk fast, run around aimlessly, and be unable to sit still. His normal relaxed giggles of delight may become high-pitched nervous laughter. And what happens soon afterward? Within a short time, he will inevitably experience a crash from his emotional high. Then comes dissatisfaction, whining, or even tears or a temper tantrum over a seemingly trivial disappointment.

Many children live on an emotional roller coaster, up one moment because they have gotten a desire fulfilled (for example, getting to play in the playground at a fast-food restaurant) and down the next (for instance, going limp in disappointment when the play time ends). These children whine, complain, and beg often and are seemingly difficult to satisfy.

What is the alternative to a child who lives in such an emotional maelstrom? It is the child who is calmly active—centered, happy, creative, and loving. Of course, every child will experience some disappointments, some anger, some frustration and discouragement, but childhood does not have to be an out-of-control period of life.

calm and compassionate children

How do *you* define happiness? Is it the temporary high you experience when you get a new car or dress or fishing rod? Is happiness the stimulation of ever louder music, ever more exciting films, more friends, parties, sports events, and thrills? Corporate advertising—which drives our media—would certainly have us think so.

Or is your definition of happiness the quiet inner calm that comes from knowing oneself, living in harmony with others, and being content in almost every circumstance? When a child is totally concentrated on doing or creating something, joyful in the process with no thought of outcome, she is calmly happy, or "in the flow." That one-pointed attention can happen while playing soccer, painting a picture, dancing on the lawn, examining a beetle, petting a kitten, learning why the sky is blue, or playing with a friend. It is a state of joy from which contentment, calmness, integrity, and compassion arise. In comparison, the overexcited agitation of a child who has too many social interactions or too many toys or too much sugar looks not so much like happiness as like one extreme of a swinging pendulum of emotions.

the challenge

Parents share with me their frustrations about their children. Some are appalled by the language, attitudes, and behavior their children bring home from school. I hear stories about premature interest in popularity and sexuality, aggression (usually physical in boys and verbal in girls), and fascination with weapons and violence. Even parents of children who have no behavior problems tell me that after their children began school, they changed—losing their natural joy and enthusiasm for life, becoming moody or depressed.

Unfortunately, many of today's children are overstimulated, oversugared, overrun with material possessions, and overscheduled. Many react to this overwhelmed state by becoming discontented, restless, and disagreeable. Some withdraw, becoming bored or cynical, listless, and world-weary at an early age. And by the time these kids reach their teens, the values their parents had worked so hard to encourage all along are ignored. Even children with strong values can be influenced by the attitudes of their peers who lack such values.

In response to these trends, many parents are looking for alternative ways to bring up their children—trying out a simpler lifestyle and looking for ways, especially for dads, to interact more with their children and have more influence on them. Parents of all different religious faiths, and many of no religious faith, are united in their desire to teach values to their children. No one wants to live in a valueless, anarchistic society. Even in a pluralistic society of multiple ethnicities and spiritual traditions, everyone can agree on universal values such as tolerance, respect, kindness, honesty, and generosity.

how children learn values

How *are* values such as kindness and respect taught to children? Of course, the most important way is by the models that parents and other adults provide. Matters of the heart are not *taught* so much as *caught*, if children are put in an environment that nurtures calmness and compassion. When children are able to be content, to tolerate differences, and to give as well as receive, it is not primarily because of religious instruction or intellectual understanding; it is a *matter of the heart.*

Loving behavior arises in large measure from an intuitive sense of connection with others. Religious instruction is traditionally thought of as the main way to pass on our values to children, but unless there is some opportunity for *experience*, that instruction is often merely an intellectual exercise. Michael Lerner, author of *Spirit Matters*, puts it this way: the "task is not to see how many texts the child can master, but how to awaken her soul to awe, wonder, and radical amazement; how to develop her recognition of others as deserving respect and as embodying God's image. . . ." Anyone can talk about values; not everyone can live out the values they talk about. Much of what passes for character education falls short because it goes from the outside in, failing to touch the heart. Children are given an overlay of lessons about right and wrong, but their inner motivation, their inner peace, their level of inner happiness—and therefore their ability to love, to give, and to take risks—is not developed.

If the heart's natural love has been suppressed, the mind can justify just about anything. Simply telling children to be peaceful does not work. One of our parents told me that her two sons were playing aggressively and fighting each other. She stopped them and explained the meaning of Jesus' admonition to turn the other cheek. "Why don't you try to be like him?"

"Okay, Mom," the older son said. As she left the room, she heard him say to his little brother, "Let's play it Mom's way. I'll be the bad guy, and you be Jesus!"

We must think more about working from the *inside out*— nurturing a child's heart—which results in behavior changes that are real and not rooted in either fear of punishment or desire for approval. The danger of raising children who behave well only for approval is apparent: as they grow older, their need for their parents' approval simply becomes a need for their peers' approval. Even worse, they can become separated from the knowledge of their own feelings and what makes them happy.

values and morals begin in the heart

One day I was sitting at my desk working, half-listening to the playground shouts from right outside my window. Noticing the innocent voices growing a bit agitated, I got up and looked outside. Four eight- and nine-year-olds were chasing a seven-year-old and had cornered him. What had begun in fun was about to turn into an unhappy situation. They were not yet doing anything hurtful, but in trying to catch the boy, their aggressive energies had gotten out of their individual control. I opened the door to intervene.

A third grade classmate of the older boys was sitting nearby, eating a snack with his back to me. Before I had even stepped outside, he resolutely stood up, approached the group, and stated loudly, "Guys, this doesn't *feel* right!" That was all it took to stop them. An eight-year-old—a peer of the group—had spontaneously done the compassionate thing, based on his inner feeling. This is the ideal we are aiming toward.

If we want our children to discover a basis for finding inner satisfaction in life, rather than seeking it in ever greater external thrills, we have to help them develop their hearts' intuition. When our hearts are open and loving, we are fearless, as well as generous and impartial. In this state of mind and heart, the body is alert, yet the heartbeat and respiration are regular and calm. This integrated experience of mind, feeling, and body is one that children can be taught to recognize and value. Some refer to it as *spirituality*. People in this state describe themselves as centered and relaxed. This is an inner experience of expansiveness, acceptance, and peace.

In the past we thought of the heart in the context of feeling as metaphorical. However, recent research is showing that the wisdom of the heart has a physiological basis. EKGs reveal that both the heart's electrical and magnetic force fields are far stronger than the brain's. Using studies done at the HeartMath Institute by Rollin McCraty, among others, Paul Pearsall (in *The Heart's Code*) and Candace Pert (in *Molecules of Emotion*) tell us that cells have intelligence and that heart cells, in particular, carry more information than we ever dreamed. Because research has only begun to explore this area of human life, we are just beginning to discover the physiological connections between the heart, the brain, and mental states of awareness. To ignore nurturing the heart aspect of the child just because it is not scientifically documented would be as foolish as it would have been to ignore the child's intellectual development before breakthroughs in brain research.

You don't need an EKG machine to see that young children readily demonstrate heart qualities. Without hesitation they will offer a lick of their ice cream cone to a stranger, laugh with delight at the sight of a bug, or put their small hands into the hands of their adult companions. As they mature, we can help them develop empathy and integrity on this foundation of open-heartedness and trust.

The results of a heart-oriented approach are profound. Just this school year, as I write, parents have sent the following two unsolicited thank-you messages to teachers.

"My daughter is a changed person. I could begin to detail the growth and peace and sense of spirit that has blossomed in her since beginning first grade, but words would not do the transformation justice."   —M. M., *parent of first grader*

"There is no better place for our son than your classroom, as he begins to piece together a framework from which to live his life. He is laying down a set of values and I am so thankful. . . . If he is able to choose peace, balance, happiness, caring, and giving, over the culturally popular version of success, you will have had a big part to play in this."
—P. G., *parent of fifth grader*

When parents and other educators visit our school, they often remark that they have never seen a school where the children are so relaxed and happy. An educator from Europe told me, after spending two weeks assisting in classrooms, that he felt the children's contentment was a by-product of teachers who work with the children "from the heart."

What does it mean to work with children "from the heart?" How does it look when teachers and parents encourage heart qualities in children? It may look quite different from classroom to classroom and from one home to another! However, if you feel the energy behind what you see happening outwardly in a calm compassionate home or a classroom, you will find great commonality. There will be a sense of acceptance and love, affirmation of strengths and positive attributes, an openness and trust. What I am describing is primarily a state of consciousness—and not a defined, rigid system of doing things. If we come from the heart, we are "in the moment," feeling what the needs of the child are and responding to those needs in the most appropriate way.

It is difficult for parents who value such ideals as sensitivity, tolerance, nonviolence, and the courage to love, to promote these values in the face of the competing messages from media and influences outside the family. But it is not impossible! A family or a teacher *can* create an environment that encourages children to develop their heart qualities and inner strength. By wisely guiding your child's experiences, it is possible to help a child become joyful, self-expressive, happy, and respectful of others without repressing or controlling him.

how you can use this book

Children who are concerned with the feelings of others, enthusiastic, and motivated to learn are children who

- Have experienced trust, respect, and loving guidance
- Are exposed to models who demonstrate high values
- Are given the *life experiences* that allow them to discover that they are happier when they think of others

My purpose in this book is to provide practical guidance for you, as parents and teachers, to provide those life experiences that will help your children learn the rewards of being calm and compassionate. Chapters 1 through 10 present ten approaches parents and teachers can use to cultivate children's compassion and calmness. Many of the suggested activities—nature outings, reading aloud, listening to music—will be familiar. However, doing them with the conscious intention of creating more love and peacefulness in your family can completely change their outcome. For example, your child probably already has a favorite doll or stuffie. You may simply look on his attachment with an amused and tolerant eye, but have you ever thought that you can help the child expand his heart's sympathies through that stuffie? You probably already listen to music with your child, too, but what would happen if you consciously selected music to uplift your child, to help him relax and focus?

Other activities will likely be new and different—for example, bringing silence into your household as a positive presence. Silence is a missing ingredient in so many children's lives, and we need silence to hear our inner selves.

calm and compassionate children

Surprisingly to most people, children thrive in and enjoy peace and quiet once they are given opportunities to experience it.

Part One, Awakening the Heart's Feeling, describes techniques that help children develop more awareness and a loving heart. Part Two, Calming Body and Mind, focuses on helping children find peace of mind and inner calm. I chose to present them in this order because you will probably already be familiar with more of the activities in Part One than in Part Two. These parts are not *steps* one and two. They all work together; start with the ideas that spark your enthusiasm. There are over ninety suggestions in the practical steps that end the chapters; some of these are bound to work for your family.

All the ideas work best when the adult leader is calm and loving and has joy to share! *Your* consciousness in sharing with your child is actually much more important than the activities themselves. It is important that you choose moments when you and your child are relaxed to use the practical steps that end the chapters. No book can substitute for the teacher or parent being fully present and attentive to the child's needs and perceptions. Also, your unconditional love is required, and children naturally put you through a lot to test that love!

Children learn best from their models—parents, teachers, and, to a degree, peers and media. Part Three, Surrounding Influences, shows you how to provide an environment conducive to calmness and compassion. Chapter 11 discusses peers, schools, and media. Finally, the last chapter gives some suggestions to all adults who influence children—

parents, grandparents, teachers, nannies, coaches—for how to *be* more calm and compassionate.

Chapter 12 is followed by self-inventories for both parents and teachers. These will help you identify areas in which you are already nurturing calmness and compassion as well as new interests you might like to explore.

Relax and have fun experimenting with the practical suggestions. You will see that calmness and compassion are not dull, but joyful and rewarding! As you do your best to parent or teach from the heart, you will find that your own spiritual development will be enhanced. Slow down, tune in to your children, and participate with them in those spheres in which heart qualities can develop; soon you'll find that your own fears, anxieties, and restless thoughts will subside as well. You will begin to discover (or rediscover) your own calmness and compassion.

Part One

Awakening the Heart's Feeling

THESE FIVE CHAPTERS are not sequential; look through the chapter titles and begin with what appeals to you. All of the approaches work together and reinforce each other. In fact, if you are more attracted to the topics in Part Two, you can start there. Go first with what feels most natural for you and your family.

When you find an activity you would like to use with your children, do not rush into it. Wait, watch, and listen for the right moment. The child's receptivity is as important as your enthusiasm.

For example, during an Education for Life workshop, I set up an "Un-Nature Trail" (from *Sharing Nature with Children*) for parents and teachers. The Un-Nature Trail elicits concentration, as the participant becomes focused on finding tiny items placed along the trail. After the three-hour workshop concluded, I noticed a parent pulling her five-year-old daughter away from her friends to go on the Un-Nature Trail. The little girl impatiently walked down the path, too restless to focus on very much. Soon the mother came to me, frustrated: "See? She just won't cooperate!" But it was not the child's fault that the mother chose a time when the girl was tired and more interested in her peers.

Although my suggestions are serious, you do not have to do them with a serious attitude! Just relax and have fun. If you are persistent, but gentle, you will find gradual changes beginning to happen both in your children and in your own perceptions of them.

Rituals are the lenses through which we see our emotional connections to each other, to a culture, and to a higher power. They are symbolic expressions of our most sacred values.

—Becky Bailey,
I Love You Rituals

CHAPTER ONE

Celebrations, Routines, and Rituals

YOU PROBABLY ALREADY have rituals that reassure and calm your child, but you may not have thought of them as rituals. When your child gets an "owie" and you kiss it, when you read a story at bedtime, or when you have pizza every Saturday night, you are creating family rituals that give your child a calming sense of stability and belonging.

A *routine* is an activity or a sequence of activities that takes place at the same time and in the same order daily or weekly. A *ritual* may be done routinely or not, but it is made a ritual by the attention and intention the participants give to it. For example, a blessing before eating may be a ritual if the family feels gratitude or reverence during the blessing, but if the blessing is said without thought or attention, it is more of a routine than a ritual. Brushing one's teeth before going to bed is a routine, but if a parent makes tooth-brushing into an episode in the war against the "cavity monsters" and plays *Star Wars* music while the kids brush, it could turn into a ritual!

A friend's mother used to amaze me with her holiday spirit. She had a little china ax she brought out to decorate the table for Washington's Birthday ("I cannot tell a lie, Father—I chopped down the cherry tree"), and she always made cherry pie. Fourth of July, Veteran's Day, birthdays of famous people—she never missed a chance to make a day into an occasion.

I thought this was sort of trite and silly, but as I got older, I realized that this celebratory spirit is fun and can be very meaningful to children. Seasonal rituals and holiday celebrations do more than create a rhythm, security, and a calm predictability: they also transmit our values. Their cyclical nature reminds us that behind change and seeming chaos there is order and calm. Seasonal rituals remind us of our connection to nature and help us appreciate that interdependence.

You will find that the aspect of a holiday that you give attention to will be embraced by your young children. For example, on Valentine's Day, I emphasized friendship in my fifth and sixth grade class. I brought in materials to make valentines for everyone, read poems about friends, and had a party with treats where children served each other drinks and food. The usual "romantic" connotations of the day and the hurt feelings that can follow disappeared, and we all enjoyed the occasion as a holiday about friendship.

At our school, each year we have certain events that children look forward to, such as making Stone Soup, school assemblies, Valentine's Day, the food bank drive, and Awards Day. Every October the kindergarten class does a play for parents, *The Big Pumpkin.* The older children love coming to see how the current year's group of five-year-olds perform, and they enjoy reminiscing about their roles when they too were "little." In the *Journal of Family Psychology* Barbara Fiese, Ph.D., writes that rituals involve "symbolic communication and convey 'this is who we are' as a group and provide continuity in meaning across generations." As the children in our school get older, they love to take on the more adult role of helping to provide that continuity to the younger children in the school.

Sometimes children turn an event into a ritual that we had not even envisioned. Our primary teacher, Karen Busch, created our Thanksgiving Stone Soup celebration. In November she reads the folk tale "Stone Soup" to her class. All the students bring vegetables from home, and the day before Thanksgiving they chop them up, add a stone, and cook "Stone Soup" that they serve to the whole school for lunch. It has become an annual event.

One year, after we finished eating I had all the students who had been in the school for seven years (kindergarten through grade six) stand up, and we took photos. Next, we had the students who had attended the school six years join them for another photo. And so on, until the whole school was standing. The following year, after we finished our pumpkin pie and I announced it was time to return to the classrooms, one of the students cried, "But aren't we going to do the thing where we stand up if we've been here the most years, and then the next most? Remember?"

"Oh, yeah!" other students joined in. "We have to do it again."

And so was born another ritual, one that reminds the students they are part of something bigger than themselves, something with continuity and worth.

One teacher celebrates Martin Luther King Jr.'s birthday with her students. She puts up a poster of King, tells them about the civil rights movement, and plays a recording of the "I Have a Dream" speech. She makes the holiday not just another day off from school, but an important time to recognize both the courage to stand up for one's principles and the dignity and freedom deserved by all. Her emphasis on this holiday makes quite an impression. One year, for an end-of-the-year present, her students got together secretly and memorized much of the speech. They practiced it during their lunch periods, and surprised her with a recitation on the last day of school. These students will always remember how it felt to recite King's stirring ideals, giving their teacher a gift that caused tears of joy to well up in her eyes.

Your family has its own religious or ethnic traditions and rituals that you probably want to pass down to your children. You may have noticed the reference to "a higher power" in the Becky Bailey quote that heads this chapter. My personal belief is that having a spiritual life contributes greatly to the development of calm compassion; however, I am sure many atheists and agnostics are calm and compassionate too! The suggestions I offer in this book can be used by anyone, of any faith, or of none.

My point of view is that there is a higher power that one can call unconditional love, the peace that passes understanding, God, Divine Mother, the Great Spirit, universal

calm and compassionate children

intelligence, Jehovah, Allah, or any other name. Religions are attempts to understand and know that universal intelligence, and each is a path to that Truth. As a saint said, "All the rivers of truth at last merge with the sea."

I believe we can access the "unknowable" through prayer and intuition, but I understand that my position is not provable, and that some readers will disagree. I do want you to understand what I mean when I occasionally use the words *God* or *spirit* as shorthand to refer to these unfathomable infinite concepts.

Regardless of whether you have a formal religious or spiritual path that you find compatible with your beliefs, you can develop meaningful family rituals relating to nature.

inventing celebrations and ceremonies

You can invent your own celebrations and ceremonies. Toby Moorhouse developed a "smudging" ritual, based on the Native American concept of smudging for cleansing and protection. If her class gets disturbed about something or if the children argue and have a hard time letting go of their animosity, she suggests a smudging. They always want to do it. She makes the event special, announcing ahead of time when it will happen. She dims the lights and begins with a song. She asks the "Great Spirit" to purify the class and to help each individual let go of bad feelings. Then she waves the smoking sage around each child's body, in front and behind, while music plays. The children love it, and it really seems to help them move on.

If you enjoy nature, you can make a nature shrine on your next camping trip or in your yard if it lends itself to it. (If you live in a city apartment and you don't go camping, see practical steps 9 and 10 at the end of this chapter.) You can use a large rock, a piece of firewood, or a log for your base. Find some flat rocks and let your child stack them three to five high, testing different configurations for stability. With enough flat stones, an older child will be able to make a taller stack in the tradition of cairns—Scottish stone piles that mark mountain peaks, trails, and graves. When you go for walks, collect special objects to place around the rocks: a dried seedpod, a beautiful bit of lichen, a colored leaf, or an abandoned wasps' nest. Seasonally, make it a ritual to clean up around the shrine and let your children arrange the objects on it. Sing a song or say a prayer.

You can celebrate the smallest event when you relate that event to the seasons. For example, you can make an occasion of the first snowdrop—because it means that spring is coming; the first azalea blossom—because it means warm weather is here; the first red leaf—to say good-night to the trees; or the first frost—because it's time for the plants and trees to go to sleep. Little rituals you and your child create around nature's cycles (perhaps just lighting a candle at dinner or decorating specially for dinner) can help children notice and feel connected to all of life and appreciate that their bodies are part of nature.

Do you live in a high-rise surrounded by pavement, with little opportunity to observe the changes in plants and animals? You can connect to nature's rhythms by observing the moon's phases (see practical step 7). Or you can make it a big deal the first time you purchase a food that symbolizes the season: strawberries for spring, watermelon for summer, pumpkins or winter squash for autumn, and nuts in their shells for winter (see practical step 8).

A celebration can be as simple as making hot cider to drink on the morning of the first frost. More elaborately, you and your child could make special place mats to use for a few days to mark the advent of each season. One easy way is to buy a large pad of paper from an art store (you'll have enough for four seasons). With your children, you can decorate each place mat simply by using markers to draw signs of the season, such as flowers, colored leaves, or snowmen. Or you can be more elaborate—cut out snowflakes or glue on pressed leaves and cover the place mats with clear contact paper. Do not just hand the materials to your children; sit down with them and make one yourself.

What makes a ritual calming and reassuring is that it is *an event meaningful to adults that children can join in.* If it is something for them to do alone, it's not a ritual or celebration—it's a child's activity. *Your presence*—talking about the day, telling a story of what you did as a child, or just listening—is the most important element.

daily routines

Daily routines are especially calming for the young child. For children younger than six or seven, seasonal celebrations seem impossibly far off and difficult to remember. Doing the same thing at the same time each day reminds them of yesterday and the day before; to them, that cycle is comparable to the cycle of seasons as adults perceive it.

A repetitive daily rhythm may sound boring to you, but children love it and thrive on it. In the *Journal of Family Psychology*, Barbara Fiese, coauthor of a review of fifty years of research on family traditions, concluded that children are both healthier and better behaved in families with predictable routines. Helen Gorman, the kindergarten teacher at Portland's Living Wisdom School, has almost the same routine every day in her class. The children have their story at the same time; they practice a letter and a sound at the same time; they have "choice time" when they finish their math activity. Weather permitting, they have snacks at the same picnic table outside every day. Within that routine there are new activities, and the children's boundaries are expanded with art, music, field trips, and more. But Helen says that when she tries to do a major change of schedule, the five-year-olds *protest* with pleas such as, "No, we can't go outside; we didn't practice counting by tens yet!" They love their routine.

Think back to the last time you had to learn something new and essential; for example, when the computer system changed at work, or when you moved and had to learn how to navigate in a completely new environment. The young child is *always* functioning at this level of adapting and learning new skills. Not only is she acquiring language, culture, and knowledge of what is and is not appropriate, but she is also constantly pushing at the edge of her abilities of gross and fine motor skills. From learning to use the doorknob, to cutting with scissors, to catching a ball, she has to apply willpower and effort to master every new skill. Normal development produces a normal and healthy state of stress—just enough to keep the child alert—and is best supported by calm and predictable rhythms of life. If the child is hurried here and there, if constant unexpected transitions happen, or especially if she does not get enough rest, the stress level becomes too high. When the stress level rises, calmness turns into frustration, crying, lack of cooperation, and sometimes hyperactivity.

Young couples who thrive on an erratic lifestyle of late nights and being on the go may be able to continue that pattern for a while with an infant. However, if they don't establish a regular routine and predictable rhythms of eating and sleeping, dressing, bathing, playing, and quiet times, their children will suffer for it. Sometimes a parent asks me for suggestions on how to get a reluctant child to get up and get dressed in the morning. But the real question is, "How do I get my child to bed early enough each night?" A well-rested child is calmer and more in control of his emotions and energy. Daily routines and rituals help children get their sleep.

transitions

In addition to establishing a regular daily routine, you can help your child to transition smoothly from one activity to the next. Transitions can be challenging for all of us, but for a young child, every transition of the day can seem momentous. Leaving home to go to school, leaving play to come to a meal, leaving Mom or Dad to go to bed—all can be threatening. To an adult who has twenty-five or more years of memories, these transitions are hardly noticeable; you know you will come home again, play the game again, wake up and have another day. For a child there is only the moment, and if he is enjoying what he is doing at that moment, ending the activity feels as though it will be permanent. Parents can help.

Before you ask a child to start something new, stop and relax for a moment. Take a deep breath, let it out slowly, and let your child know that a change is about to happen. Especially if your child is quietly focusing on something, you do not want to jerk him away from it without warning. If you respectfully acknowledge his concentration, he learns that the ability to focus is valued: "I see you're going to be able to build a big tower the way you are working on it, but we have to take your sister to school. You may play for another minute; then we are going to put on our coats and go." Do your best to stop and watch your little one at play during that minute. This process will be well worth your trouble for the child's developing sense of self-respect and autonomy.

Some children who rebel at leaving what they are doing will respond to a challenge: "I bet you can't get your coat on and get out to the car as fast as I can!" A parent of a kindergartener told me that challenging her daughter's willpower made all the difference in getting her cooperation to leave the house and get in the car, because it became a game. However, for children who are more feeling-oriented than will-oriented, acknowledging and respecting their feelings as I described in the previous paragraph will probably work better.

What helps most is a regular routine of meals, bathtime, and bedtime, each at its own regular time, with fun and comforting rituals to smooth the way through the transitions. The thought of adding anything to your daily routine may be overwhelming. However, if you establish little rituals and are consistent day after day, life with children will be easier in the long run. Having consistent routines with meaningful rituals may not turn your children into little angels, but you will definitely notice a difference in their ability to move from one activity to another.

singing

One of our routines at school includes singing the song "Go with Love" by Donald Walters at the end of the school day in kindergarten and primary grades, especially if we are leaving for a holiday or school break. The words to "Go with Love" are profound, and the tune is light and uplifting.

Go with love; may joyful blessing
Speed you safely on your way.
May God's light expand within you
May we be one in that light someday.

Singing this song is also our ritual when a student leaves for a trip or moves away. We gather in a circle with the departing one in the middle and sing it together.

This song has helped the children through times of grief, too. One morning Marie, a parent in my school, stopped by my office. "Ian may be a little subdued or grouchy today," she said. "His beloved kitty, Abby, died yesterday."

"How old was Abby?" I asked.

"Ten! She's been around his whole life, and she slept with him often. He was just in anguish, until we buried her. And then do you know what he did?"

"What?"

"He said we should sing 'Go with Love,' and so his sister and he and I stood around the grave and sang it. That seemed to give him more comfort than anything else."

It wasn't just the song's words that were reassuring to Ian, but also the familiar ritual of singing it at a leave-taking. Singing the song reminded him of other times he had sung it at separations—and the fact that he had successfully survived them. If you establish rituals with words and songs meaningful to your family, you will be building inner resources that your child can call on later just as Ian did. You could sing the first lines of "Oh, What a Beautiful Morning," as you sit down to breakfast or, if you're not a morning person, "Kumbaya" or Paul Simon's "St. Judy's Comet" when you get ready for bed.

developing family rituals and routines

Rituals in the morning can consist of waking to a song sung by you or to a little dialogue routine, such as:

You say, "Who's my favorite four-year-old? Who can it be? Why, here he is fast asleep. Is it Joey? Is it Jenny? Is it Jack? Or is it Jill?"

And the child replies, "No, it's Jason!"

And then you kiss his cheek or tickle his feet.

Bedtime rituals are especially important; you can find suggestions about them in chapter 5, practical step 11, and chapter 6, practical step 3.

Rituals for arriving or leaving home are fun. When you get in the car and buckle up, have everyone close their eyes, take a deep breath, and mentally bless everyone you'll meet that day. When I was a classroom teacher, one of our little field-trip rituals was to stop the car in the driveway on our way out, close our eyes, and visualize our trip surrounded by harmony and joy. Not until everyone in the car was peaceful (meaning their breath became quiet and slow) would we leave the campus. This routine gave us a great intention for the trip, and it motivated the children to calm down.

You can make up your own little "going and coming" rituals. As you leave and return home from running errands, you might say together: "To market, to market, to buy a fat pig," and, "Home again, home again, jiggidy jig." When your children return home on their own, you could open the back door with a flourish and bow to each child, saying "Welcome home, Sir Henry; welcome home, Lady Ella."

When the children are little they might like to bow and curtsy for fun, saying, "Thank you, Mother dear."

I read aloud the *Not-Just-Anybody Family* series by Betsy Byars to one of my classes. In these novels, one child always says good-bye, not only to people and animals, but to inanimate objects. We started that little routine ourselves when we left for a town trip, and one student, Narani, said good-bye to the trees, the buildings, and the play equipment. We laughed, and several other students began to imitate her. It was a great focus and source of closure as we left one place for the next. Leaving a campground, for example, the children looked for places and items they had interacted with and said, "Good-bye, picnic table where we ate; good-bye, campsite; good-bye, little ground squirrels; good-bye, hemlock tree."

Rituals around food are natural. For my stepchildren, their dad, and me, Saturday morning pancakes were a great family sharing time. No matter what else was happening on the weekend, we could look forward to Dad's cooking Saturday breakfast and having that mealtime together before we got busy with other activities. You probably already have routines around meals, such as sitting in certain spots or setting the table a certain way.

Beginning the meal with a blessing or an expression of gratitude calms everyone down before you start to eat. Children love to learn and say a blessing or a toast. You can also simply go around the table and each share one thing about the day that you are grateful for. Waiting until everyone is quiet and attentive before you begin is an important part of this ritual. And do not forget routines around cleanup.

calm and compassionate children

Make it fun. Have children take their plates to the kitchen to "feed the dishwasher."

Daily rituals give children memories for a lifetime. I remember fondly how my father brought me a little glass of orange juice each school day when he woke me up in the morning. It did not necessarily make me get up any more eagerly, but the predictability of this daily gesture made me feel secure in his love.

PRACTICAL STEPS

1. WHEN ANYONE in the family reaches a milestone (finishing kindergarten, a promotion at work, making that first goal in a soccer game), turn an ordinary dinner into a celebration. If you don't have time to cook a whole meal, pick up an entree the family enjoys and add a salad and make a dessert. Let your child help (or do it alone if he is old enough) put out a fabric table cloth, set the table with your best dishes, and make a centerpiece. Light candles, say a blessing or words of appreciation, and toast the honoree.

2. ADOPT A BEDTIME RITUAL that suits your family. Elements may include calming music, prayers, back or foot rubs, read-aloud or sing-along time, cuddling, and sharing the day's highlights (see practical step 11 in chapter 5). Start and end the ritual in the same way and at the same time each night for a feeling of security and predictability.

3. LET YOUR CHILD decorate the table for dinner with a centerpiece made from whatever is seasonal; for example, autumn leaves for fall, oranges and apples in winter, red hearts and candles in February, or red, white, and blue crepe paper for July Fourth.

4. WHILE you are cooking, help your child compose a poem or song to begin the evening meal. A song celebrating some sign of the season that you observed that day is perfect.

5. SEARCH your own childhood memories. Do any of them involve celebrations or yearly rituals? Can you adapt one of these or create a new one that suits your present lifestyle? Ask your children for input; sometimes they come up with great ideas of how to contribute to an event. After you try it, come back together and talk about how it went and how it did or did not meet your expectations. Sometimes debriefing an activity is more valuable than the activity itself, as new insights may arise.

6. DO A WEB SEARCH on the Indian art of mandala and rangoli, and look at the pictures for inspiration. Using colored sands or different colors of legumes, make a mandala on a large round tray to display at a special event. Or let the children use colored chalk to create rangolis on the driveway to welcome guests.

7. BUY A CALENDAR that shows the phases of the moon. Each night as part of your bedtime ritual, put a sticker on the day and count how many days remain until the full moon. Make a ritual for each full moon. This could be going for an evening walk together to admire the moon when it's visible. If it's cloudy or rainy, you can light candles at home and read a book like Jane Yolen's *Owl Moon* or *The Moon Book* by Gail Gibbons. On earlier nights in the cycle, read *Wait Till the Moon Is Full* by Margaret Wise Brown.

8. FIND A FARMERS' MARKET or roadside fruit or vegetable stand that you can easily travel to. Make it a point to take your child there two or three times during the harvest season. Involve your child with selecting the produce by teaching him what you look for in each item (color, softness, smell, weight).

9. JOIN with another like-minded family for seasonal or spiritual celebrations if you do not participate in any organized religious or spiritual group that fulfills this function. Some families celebrate each equinox and solstice, recognizing the importance of nature's rhythms in our lives. Elements you might include: lighting candles, music, movement (see chapter 7), a prayer, a poem, decorations, food.

10. READ *I'm in Charge of Celebrations* by Byrd Baylor for ideas on making celebrations out of natural events (see appendix 3). You can read it aloud to your children, but in my experience you will be the one inspired by it to take more notice of what's going on around you and to share that with your children.

Few are altogether blind and
deaf to the sweet looks and
voices of nature. There is a love
of wild Nature in everybody.

—John Muir

CHAPTER TWO
Nature Awakens Feeling

MY FOURTH AND FIFTH GRADE class loved to be outdoors. We often did our reading outside and sometimes took hikes. But there were two or three children in the class who weren't receptive to the subtle messages of the natural world. They were too busy running, yelling, and whacking at the plants with sticks.

I decided to read aloud *The Tracker*, by Tom Brown Jr., an expert on wilderness survival and tracking (see appendix 3). The story describes his early training with his best friend and his best friend's grandfather, an Apache medicine man. The book is just macho enough to appeal to the "all-boy" types in the class, but also communicates deep respect for nature and for the importance of self-control in order to be quiet and observe. The children loved the story and began emulating the book's characters: for example, getting as close as possible to animals or birds without disturbing them. This appealed enormously to the children who formerly had trouble being still in nature; they enjoyed using their will to challenge themselves.

I have wonderful memories of special times with those nine- and ten-year-olds. I remember a recess when the entire class spontaneously lay down on the pavement in the parking lot to watch cloud formations and insisted that I join them. Another great experience was the time we drove to a nearby creek to picnic, but it started to rain. I was all for going back to the classroom, but no; the children reminded me that the kids in the book wouldn't let a little rain or snow stop *them*.

We went down by the stream and spread out to find dry spots. Crouching under banks and trees, we ate our lunches silently, watching the rain fall on the water. We were all so content to just *be* there in communion with the nature around us; it was one of those unforgettable life events that cannot be planned. The only word I can think of to describe how it felt is *sacred*.

Nothing surpasses the power of nature to relax and engage children in a way that calms them and opens their hearts. Children love to go outside and relate to the natural world around them. I have a friend who teaches in a private school. She has the opportunity to introduce her class to many activities we might label as spiritual: guided visualizations, prayer beads, healing prayers, and art while listening to sacred music. But when she asked the children to share the time they felt closest to God, one little boy did not recall any of these activities. He wrote, "I felt close to God the day we hiked up to the top of the big hill and saw the hawk flying over the valley." Whether or not you believe in a higher power, we all can agree that there are realities other than our own—in a pod of whales, a herd of elephants, an ant colony. "Nature introduces children to the idea—to the knowing—that they are not alone in the world, and that realities and dimensions exist alongside their own," Richard Louv explains in *Last Child in the Woods: Saving Our Children from Nature-Deficit Disorder.*

Shakespeare put it poetically: "One touch of Nature makes the whole world kin." When children have the chance to be aware in nature, they almost always feel that kinship, and feeling kinship with any form of life increases one's compassion.

our ultimate nature experience

When I taught at the Living Wisdom School near Nevada City, California, I heard about a local site where ladybugs hibernated. On the banks of Humbug Creek (named during the Gold Rush, not for the bugs!), the place was said to be teeming with these beetles in very early spring. I read a book about ladybugs to the class, and we decided on a field trip to see them for ourselves.

The day of our trip we talked about what it might be like to see so many ladybugs in one place; the class was very excited about it. I led a visualization asking them to close their eyes and imagine the ladybugs, sending them love and telling them we wanted to visit them, and apologizing and blessing any we might accidentally step on. (Whether or not you believe in any type of interspecies communication, this type of exercise is valuable for children: it develops their ability to see another point of view—a first step to compassion.)

At the beginning of our hike at Humbug Creek, some students were wildly unobservant: running down the trail, talking loudly, oblivious of all they passed. Luckily the destination was a half-mile away, which gave the children time to expend some of their pent-up energy physically and to calm down before we reached the hibernation site. After hiking about fifteen minutes, children began to notice a few ladybugs on plants. We stopped. I asked the children to walk in silence and to point to any ladybug they spotted. This silent focus brought them into their centers as observers.

Suddenly they found a log *covered* with ladybugs. And then, looking closer to the stream, we realized that the rust-colored rocks we saw were really gray rocks covered with beetles, and some weren't rocks at all but mounds of ladybugs! It was astonishing. Piles of ladybugs in the shade were completely dormant, but the ones in the sun were teeming masses.

We were amazed. We realized that we were witnessing something none of us had ever seen before and that many people would never see. It was, as kids say, awesome. The children moved slowly and carefully to avoid crushing the beautiful insects. Some of the nine-year-olds preferred just to look, not wanting to touch the beetles. But others loved picking up handfuls and letting them crawl up their arms and into their hair. Soon we were all laughing as ladybugs tickled our skin.

All year long we reminisced about "the ladybug hike." The children experienced a deep connection with nature that day. Even nine years later, unexpectedly seeing a student who had been in that class, I asked the then eighteen-year-old, "Do you remember the ladybugs?"

"Ohhh!" She drew her breath in and smiled at the memory. "Oh, yes. I'll never forget."

Whether it's watching a hawk soar overhead or picking up a mound of ladybug beetles, nature can awaken awe and reverence in the human heart. Reading books on our relationship to the natural world and watching nature videos are great activities, but they can never have the power to move children's hearts that real-life experiences have.

touching the future

Not every nature experience will be this magical, of course. I remember another group of students about the same age. Their teacher, a parent, and I took them to Bend, Oregon, to Pioneer Days at the High Desert Museum. The next day the teacher led us on a hike along a river where she hoped we would see ospreys feeding. Some students whined that they did not want to take a walk; they were "too tired." These few continued to complain they were bored even after seeing the osprey building its nest. Yet their time in nature had subtle calming effects that they did not recognize, but that we observed by how much more relaxed they became by the end of the hike.

You never know what experience in nature will touch a child's heart. It may be on the edge of a mountaintop with an exhilarating view, or it may be a quiet moment watching a mother bird feed her babies. My friend Kiya Gornik recently graduated from Lewis and Clark College in Portland. She was my student in fifth and sixth grades, and we have kept in touch since. She majored in biology and plans to go on for her master's degree, either to teach or to do research. She was selected to do a semester study at Woods Hole Institute of Oceanography, which involved six weeks on a ship in the Pacific. She also worked for two summers at the Earthwatch Research Station in the Bahamas.

I told Kiya that I would not have predicted she would become a biologist. I remember her as a girl who loved the arts, first and foremost. She was very musical, loved to sing, and loved to act.

Kiya replied, "Well, it was in your class that my interest in biology began."

I did not even remember any biology until Kiya reminded me of our unit on birds. Besides our classroom learning, we spent a day observing a bird-banding project, walking the nets and extricating and banding tiny warblers.

The children were thrilled when we discovered a pair of orioles building a nest in a huge ponderosa pine beside our classroom. From the library we had access to the roof and a "bird's-eye view" of the oriole nest. Almost every day we took our binoculars and our lunches up to the roof and watched the female sitting on the eggs and the male bringing food. Not too many days after the babies hatched, we saw the first head pop up out of the nest, beak wide open.

We felt like proud parents when the babies finally fledged just before school closed for the summer. Although we all loved our bird family, Kiya was the most excited of all the students. The next year Kiya visited my classroom to tell me she had seen another pair of orioles near her house. Although Kiya is probably the only one in that class who has gone on to make biology or ecology her profession, I suspect that every student who was part of that experience still remembers our rooftop bird-watching. Such experiences speak to the heart and help us to relax into our interconnectedness with all life.

if you live in the city or suburbs

You don't have to live in a rural environment to have a powerful experience in nature. Richard Louv writes in *Last Child in the Woods*:

> *A trip to REI to get just the right camping equipment for a two-week vacation in Yosemite is not a prerequisite, or for that matter, any substitute for more languid natural pastimes that can be had in the backyard.*
>
> *The dugout in the weeds or leaves beneath a backyard willow, the rivulet of a seasonal creek, even the ditch between a front yard and the road—all of these places are entire universes to a young child. Expeditions to the mountains or national parks often pale, in a child's eyes, in comparison with the mysteries of the ravine at the end of the cul de sac.*

Nature is everywhere, even in empty lots of big cities and corners of suburbs, but you do have to stay alert and look for opportunities to find and appreciate those slices of nature with your child. One morning at our school, the primary class took turns watching baby swallows in a nest under an eave. We set up a step ladder so each one could climb up and see. Every child was rapt with attention. The fact that a parent spent more than an hour holding the ladder as each of us had a few minutes to watch made a powerful statement to the children about the importance we place on life.

A great nature activity you can do as long as you have some shrubs, a patch of grass, a vacant lot or even a ditch or swale, is a *micro-hike*. As described by Joseph Cornell in *Sharing Nature with Children*, you give your child a magnifying glass and a piece of string four or five feet long. You take one, too! Span your strings "over the most interesting ground you can find."

Get down on your hands and knees and, keeping your eyes no higher than one foot above the ground, crawl along your string examining everything you can find. How many kinds of plants are there? What are the insects doing? What are the colors like? Would this hike look the same if it were raining? At the end of the string share with each other what you discovered, then trade places and take each other's hikes. This helps the hurried child slow down as he attempts to discover all the things you saw along your string.

On warm spring days, I used to take my class outside to read silently on the tiny lawn. If children's attention strayed from reading to the clouds or to insects crawling nearby, I smiled encouragement as long as they did not talk. They all loved to read, but calm contemplation of some aspect of nature is rare in this age of electronic entertainment.

Our kindergarten teacher regularly takes her children on nature walks through our suburban neighborhood to

calm and compassionate children

collect beautiful gifts of the season they find alongside the sidewalks and streets. Each child chooses one gift of nature to bring back, such as an unusual leaf, an acorn, or a dandelion blossom. Then they arrange nature's offerings beautifully on their nature table.

If you live in an apartment building surrounded by pavement, you can still connect with nature by providing food and water for the birds outside one of your windows. However, getting your child into green space is still important.

In a study published in *Environment and Behavior*, Nancy Wells and her colleague, Gary Evans, found that a relative abundance of green landscape bolsters "children's resilience against stress or adversity." Andrea Faber Taylor and Frances Kuo, researchers at the Human Environment Research Lab sponsored by the University of Illinois at Urbana-Champaign, found "that spending time in ordinary 'green' settings—such as parks, farms or grassy backyards—reduces symptoms of ADHD [Attention Deficit and Hyperactivity Disorder] when compared to time spent at indoor playgrounds and man-made recreation areas of concrete and asphalt." Taylor and Kuo's studies showed this to be true "regardless of the child's age, gender, family income, geographic region or severity of diagnosis," as reported in *Psychology Today*. My guess is that results would be exactly the same for children who have *not* been diagnosed with ADHD—every child's ability to focus is improved by being in nature.

Numerous other studies document the positive effects of being in nature. In *Last Child in the Woods*, Richard Louv reports in depth on this topic and suggests solutions for the dwindling exposure to nature today's children are getting as they spend more and more time indoors watching TV or playing with electronic games. He writes, "In nature, a child finds freedom, fantasy, and privacy, a place distant from the adult world, a separate peace."

calming down and paying attention

Encouraging your children to explore outside and engage in the fantasy play that children tend to do in natural settings is a step in the right direction. If there are safety concerns about ill-intentioned adults or older children, do your best not to forbid your children access to natural settings; instead, go with them. Take a chair and a book, and park yourself within hearing range. Let them spend time playing, but also make it a point to direct their attention. Unstructured time in nature is great, but children also need help to develop their senses and their powers of observation to discover nature's wonders.

Helping your children have an experience of peace and discovery outdoors will flow better if you prepare them for it. Children who are not helped first to calm down for a nature experience will be like the members of my class who ran wildly down the trail whacking everything with sticks. To create a meaningful nature experience, use these four steps:

Take only one child at a time, or a couple of siblings. If you take a group of children, they will be much more interested in each other than in the natural world around them. With a group, the experience we had by the river in Bend is more usual than the picnic in the rain.

Choose a quiet place where you will not have the distractions of other people or noise so you can commune with nature. You don't have to be in the wilderness! It can be in a park or your backyard, as long as people are not too close.

Allow time to decompress and establish a comfort zone with the child *before* you ask for quiet observation or introspection. A child's receptivity is greatly enhanced when adults help her to calm down before the experience. Begin with some vigorous exercise; take a bike ride or run part of the way to the spot you are headed for. Listen to what the child wants to talk about.

Then help her focus her attention by pointing out details in a rock, a plant, or the trees. Next, engage the child's concentration by asking her to point out an oval leaf or a spotted pebble, to count how many colors of tree trunks she can see, or another detail *you* observe (see how this gets you to be more fully present, too?). When the child is able to pay attention to one thing at a time, you are ready to try a micro-hike or one of the focused activities in the following practical steps.

PRACTICAL STEPS

1. TAKE A MICRO-HIKE as described in the chapter or do a "silent bird count." (These activities and the next come from Joseph Cornell's book *Sharing Nature with Children*; see appendix 4.) Sit quietly and listen for different bird songs for three to six minutes, depending on the child's age. Sit back to back and avoid looking at each other while you listen; the mind will quiet down as the attention becomes focused on listening. Silently count how many you hear. At the end, see if you counted the same number.

2. "MEET A TREE." This one requires a wooded area, but even your neighborhood can work if there are lots of trees. Blindfold the child and walk him in circles, then to a tree you have preselected. Ask him to hug the tree, feel for lichen, moss, or insects, put his cheek next to its bark, listen to its trunk, and talk to it *silently*. Give him as much time as he wants to explore. Then lead him away from the tree, ten or fifteen yards or more, and remove the blindfold. Ask him to find his tree! Some children feel such a relationship to their trees that they will want to visit them time and time again.

3. ASK A CHILD to *find* something; for example, four objects of different shapes, three different-colored leaves, a rock with a stripe on it. Providing a task so specific gets the child focused quickly. After she has accomplished the goal, she will probably become observant and calm enough to enjoy just being outside exploring.

4. FIND PLACES to take long walks or hikes. Ideally, get a comfortable backpack child carrier and start when your child is an infant. Notice that even a baby's mood often improves as soon as you are outside. The human body responds to the natural world that sustains it.

5. TAKE A WALK around the neighborhood after a rain and look for "diamonds" on spider webs and droplets of "fairy nectar" on leaves. My friend Lorna's young daughter loves to do this. You may also find worms out on rainy-day walks. Let your children examine them as long as they want.

6. TAKE VACATIONS in natural surroundings. If your children are old enough, try camping, a dude ranch, a bicycle tour, or a rafting trip.

7. IN WINTER, hang bird feeders near your windows and obtain a bird-identification book. Discover the personalities of the different species.

8. IF YOUR CHILD ENJOYS reading and writing, make a tree field guide together as a summer or fall project. Collect and press leaves and make a simple book; for older kids who like research, include facts about each variety. Help them tune in to the characteristics of each tree by giving it a name of their own choosing.

9. IF YOU GARDEN, give your child a place to plant whatever he likes. If you have never gardened and especially if you have only a tiny space, you can easily make your child a garden as small as one foot by two feet by following the New Square Foot Garden method, popularized by Mel Bartholomew (see appendix 5). If you have no yard but you do have a deck or balcony, you can grow patio tomatoes and lettuce in containers. If you have no sun, plant shade plants such as astilbe, ferns, or impatiens.

Each time we read a book,
we go on a journey. And as with
all journeys, books change
us and bring us back to our
deeper selves.

—Patricia MacLachlan, author of
Sarah, Plain and Tall

CHAPTER THREE

The Power of Story

OUR ANCESTORS were telling stories long before the invention of theater, novels, or film. Why is storytelling so important to us? Stories not only entertain, but they also embody our history, our aspirations, and the values of our culture. They also may depict the ideals we wish our children to adopt or the villainy we wish them to avoid. Stories can inspire feelings of honor and nobility, expanding our horizons from the particular to the universal. Like nature, stories are a springboard to compassion because they stimulate feeling and open the heart.

Although stories are not *direct* experience, they can evoke real emotions. Stories of adventure, courage, and heroic and compassionate acts are felt deeply by children. A wonderful way to share our values with our children is through the tales of both real and fictional characters. Peggy Jenkins writes in *The Joyful Child*, "Good stories entertain, inform, provide vicarious insights, help solve problems, stir to action, change attitudes, present high ideals . . . and develop a positive expectancy of life."

When parents take time to read aloud, children are touched not only by the stories, but also by their parents' love. Children crawl onto our laps for a story, bodies snug against our own, and we go on a journey together. If we meet perils and evil characters—whether the big bad wolf or Mordred—it is in the context of our comforting touch and warmth. When we finish a great book and close it, there is almost always a silent pause for a few heartbeats. In an article for the *International Journal of Children's Spirituality*, Darlene L. Witte-Townsend calls that silent pause, "a place of transcendence. . . . A connection is made there in the silence."

After that heart-to-heart connection, produced by your voice sharing the story, is the perfect time to ask questions that will help your child reflect: Would you have done the same thing? If you wrote the story, would you make the ending different? Why? What do you think made the villainous character act that way? What qualities did the main character have that helped him or her? Uplifting stories about people who conquer challenges and do noble deeds thrill us all. But children and youth especially benefit from such stories because they are looking for role models to imitate.

Spiritual traditions pass down truth through stories, such as Native American creation stories, the parables of the New Testament, and the Hindu epic *Mahabharata* (containing the *Bhagavad Gita*). When we are told that we should be wary of some attractive person because he is like Coyote, we understand instantly that there is potential for deception, tricks, or ulterior motives. The simple directive "Treat

calm and compassionate children

everyone as your neighbor" is good advice, but the story of the Good Samaritan, who stopped to help a stranger by the roadside, has the power to touch our hearts.

The *Mahabharata* is full of examples of individuals giving up their personal desires for integrity or virtue. The value of loyalty is taught vividly to generations of Indians through the story of Yudhisthira's attempt to enter heaven with his dog. When the gatekeeper of heaven says dogs cannot enter, Yudhisthira, though weary and ready to be done, refuses to abandon the one who had been loyal to him through all his struggles. Then the dog transforms into the god, Indra, who tells Yudhisthira that this was his last test, and he has now achieved enlightenment.

As cultures pass down truths through story, families can do the same. Dad's story of the time he broke Grandma's vase—and how he wishes he could go back and own up to it immediately instead of suffering for a week before he was found out—is not only instructive, but tremendously fascinating to his kids. Children want to hear family stories, time and time again. I never tired of hearing about the time my father hid behind the couch when his older sister had a date. When she discovered him there, she boxed his ears, and the next morning he woke up with his face red and swollen. Both he and his sister were horrified. Later, they realized he had the mumps! I learned that it is mean to spy on your older sister and equally mean to slap your brother.

reading aloud

Carefully selected children's literature, as well as cultural and family stories, can convey your values and beliefs. Fantasy stories of the epic battles of good and evil, such as the Lord of the Rings trilogy, the Narnia Chronicles, and the *Tale of Despereaux*, give children heroes and heroines worth emulating. There are also stories of courageous and heroic modern characters such as Dicey in *Homecoming*, by Cynthia Voigt, for older readers. Animal stories touch the hearts of younger children just as pets and stuffies do (see chapter 4). Classics, such as E. B. White's *Charlotte's Web*, and newer animal stories, such as Lobel's *Frog and Toad* series, convey sweetness, compassion, and true friendship.

Reading aloud provides a shared experience between the child and the adult reader. Unfortunately, many parents perceive reading aloud as a bedtime activity for only the very young. Parents give it up as the child learns to read on his own, and they miss the opportunity to share their ideals in an indirect way just when the child is most vulnerable to influences outside the home. For example, including your teenagers when your family reads *The Education of Little Tree* can touch them deeply and convey love, loyalty, and appreciation of nature's rhythms at a time when directly mentioning those ideals would make your teens shrug, groan, or roll their eyes.

Sharon Taylor, whose son and daughter I taught, asked me a couple of times for recommendations of good read-alouds for the whole family to take on their weeklong camping trips. It was their vacation tradition: after dinner, the extended family sat around the campfire, sharing the book journey together. They read aloud together at home too. Significantly, Sharon shared with me that after her children reached school age, "Nearly all of our discussions on serious subjects were brought about through the books we read together." They continued this tradition right through the teenage years, until the kids left home.

I unexpectedly saw Maura, one of my former students, at a convenience store where we both were waiting in line at the register. A senior in high school, she had been in my class in sixth grade, five years before. I had read Wilson Rawls's *Summer of the Monkeys* to her class. Even though the ending is a bit trite and predictable, the story is so heartwarming and evokes so much laughter that I love to read it aloud.

Maura and I greeted each other with pleasure, not having seen each other in a couple of years. Then she asked, first thing, "Read *Summer of the Monkeys* lately?" I laughed, and she did too. Our shared laughter was not only at the memory of the humorous scenes in the book, but also an appreciation of the touching experiences of the struggles and love in the main character's family. From age eleven to age sixteen is a big gap, but the feelings and ideals this story evoked in Maura were still so vivid that she spoke of it after half a decade!

The popular media does not offer many examples of loving, brave, and noble characters, but you can find them in children's literature. Children will inevitably play pretend games based on the stories that they know; they imitate the main characters in the movies they see and the books they hear. So why not give them stories with characters you want them to imitate?

books versus movies

You may be thinking that your favorite movie inspires your children just as a book does. Film is one of my favorite art forms too. But watching a good movie with your child does not replace reading a book. For one thing, the pace of a book is different; it unfolds over a series of evenings, which extends the child's anticipation and openness to absorbing it. A huge difference—maybe outside the scope of this book, but worth mentioning—is that children who are read to are highly motivated to learn to read and become better readers. One factor in their better comprehension is their practice in imagining scenes and events described verbally. This ability to visualize is a characteristic of good readers, and the inability to picture what is described by words is correlated with poor reading comprehension.

Dr. Carla Hannaford explains in *Smart Moves*, "[As you read to a child] they are elaborating internal pictures, and emotions connect to their already acquired understanding. They are actively forming new nerve networks. When you have finished reading the book, the child immediately says: 'read it again,' and 'again' and 'again'! The repetition allows them to elaborate and myelinate new nerve paths." (Myelin is the fatty tissue that enables the impulses to travel faster down a neural pathway stimulated by new learning.) We adults tire of reading a story again, but by repeating it over and over, the connections made between neurons are permanently stored in the brain.

An important aspect of reading aloud is that the child hears the story through you, through your voice. Your voice is an important part of your offspring's childhood. Studies have shown that even the unborn child in the womb responds differently to the voices of father and mother and other voices. While it may be fun to listen together to recorded books, the experience is not the same as it is for the child to hear the story through the channel of your familiar voice with its unique tones and overtones.

The film experience, although it can be profound, provides much less opportunity for sharing than reading a book together. When you read aloud to your children, you can see confusion, fear, or joy in their eyes. You can stop and ask questions, offer reassurances, learn their concerns, and explain parts of the story that they do not comprehend.

getting started

When choosing books to read aloud, *always* read the book first yourself and be sure it inspires you! Your enthusiasm and interest in the story is absolutely conveyed in your voice and attitude as you read. For it to be an engaging read-aloud, it must have at least a certain amount of action, suspense, and entertaining dialogue. To build a foundation of listening for the more complex stories you want to share, first choose books that are exciting and fast-paced.

The most important factor in a successful read-aloud experience is the selection of the book. Although an average book can be interesting to your child if you, yourself, are enthusiastic and interested, nothing redeems a weak story or poor writing. Some great books are not the best read-alouds because they have long descriptive passages, or because the pace is not suited to reading aloud. The books *Island of the Blue Dolphins* by Scott O'Dell and *A Wrinkle in Time* by Madeleine L'Engle fall into this category. This is not to say that a child who has been regularly read to over the years will not enjoy these as read-alouds, but if you are *not* in the habit of reading with your children, start with books that will engage them right away with suspense and a fast pace.

One reason parents stop reading to their children when the children begin to read for themselves may be that it is harder to choose a book. You cannot judge a chapter book just by thumbing through it as you can a picture book. Because parents seem to need more help with these, I will focus on chapter-book read-alouds for children in the practical steps, beginning with a few that are appropriate for the whole family. In appendix 3 you will also find listed a few beautiful picture books and many other good books to read aloud for various ages.

If you are a parent of children from seven to eleven years old who are unaccustomed to listening to stories, I recommend beginning with a book that has short chapters, such as Bruce Coville's *Jeremy Thatcher, Dragon Hatcher*, or Dick King-Smith's *Babe, the Gallant Pig*. Elizabeth Speare's *Sign of the Beaver* is a suspenseful and engaging story for children around nine and older. These books may not be great literature, but they have heart and really engage children who are not used to listening.

If you have not already developed the habit of reading aloud to your children, do everything you can to set the stage so that your children will be open to listening. Certainly, do not interrupt them to read when they are having a great time doing something else. Choose a time when they are receptive—before bed works well. Make a treat such as popcorn or hot chocolate or chai so they will have something to do while they listen. Cozy pillows and dim lighting may also create a listening mood.

When your children have learned to listen and to trust that you will choose stories they like, you can begin to read books that are more challenging. After you have read the ones you like from my recommendations, you can find more by consulting three other good resources: the Living Wisdom School websites, the Chinaberry Book Catalog, and Jim Trelease's *Read-Aloud Handbook*, now in its sixth edition. Jim Trelease's choices are almost always very engaging stories that children enjoy listening to; he knows what makes a good read-aloud.

At the Living Wisdom School websites, teachers often post their favorite uplifting books; you may find some there that turn out to be your favorites. Although the Chinaberry Book Catalog does not focus on read-alouds, I include it because of their care in selecting books that convey noble values. They have titles for every age, including books for parents.

Children just love to hear a story. Writer Eudora Welty said, "Listening children know stories are *there*. When their elders sit and begin, children are just waiting and hoping for one to come out, like a mouse from its hole." The wise parent or teacher responds to this natural yearning with entertaining stories that depict love, courage, compassion, and joy. The stirring ideals generated by great stories produce a reservoir of aspiration that your children can draw on throughout their lives.

It is not complicated; go to your local library or bookstore today; get several of the books and read them yourself. Begin reading aloud just as soon as you find one you love. As your children are drawn in, you will quickly experience the benefits of reading to your kids, including their growing ability to calm down and listen!

READ-ALOUDS FOR THE WHOLE FAMILY

These books have themes and language that young children can hear, and yet enough adventure and suspense that older children can enjoy them too. Although the first three are not as rich as some others on the read-aloud list in appendix 3, any one of them is an excellent start if your children are not in the habit of listening to you read aloud.

Jeremy Thatcher, Dragon Hatcher, by Bruce Coville. A matchless read-aloud, this story combines the ever-popular dragon theme with a realistic contemporary setting. *Jeremy Thatcher* will capture your children's attention with short chapters and lots of suspense. Jeremy learns to expand his sympathies and to see his little dragon as a real being, not merely his possession.

Babe, the Gallant Pig, by Dick King-Smith. As entertaining as the movie is, the book is even better. If your child has trouble having empathy for animals or other people, this one is a good one to help open the heart.

The Tale of Despereaux, by Kate DiCamillo. The adventures of the endearing mouse, Despereaux. Surrounded by small-minded mice, he dares to follow his heart. A sweet tale of the triumph of love and sincerity over meanness of the heart. It's a little long for a very first read-aloud, but a great second or third. The author speaks straight to the reader, making it immediate.

Little House in the Big Woods and all of this series by Laura Ingalls Wilder. Great read-alouds; classics that deserve their status. Although the characters are all sisters, the father is a good role model for boys, and any child can identify with the sometimes naughty main character. A friend who read these to her seven-year-old daughter said her eleven-year-old son listened and enjoyed them too.

FOR MORE SOPHISTICATED LISTENERS (AT LEAST NINE YEARS AND OLDER)

After you have developed the art of reading aloud and your child has developed the art of listening, you can graduate to more challenging books with longer chapters and more advanced vocabulary.

Summer of the Monkeys, by Wilson Rawls. In this book, a boy whose masculine identity depends on his hunting needs to capture some monkeys alive in order to claim award money. His exploits with his grandfather and his dog in trying to catch the monkeys are hilarious. When he finally catches the monkeys, it is through compassion rather than tricks and wiles.

Wise Child, by Monica Furlong. The heroine lives with an herbalist who comes to be suspected as a witch when tragedies strike the town. There is a close friendship between a girl (the main character) and a boy (her cousin). This book, especially popular for girls in the nine-to-fourteen age group, shows the lure of luxury and the contrasting inner joy of a simple life. One that appeals more to boys (ages seven to ten) is Frances Hodgkin Burnett's *The Lost Prince*, but it is a bit old-fashioned. Both of these are best for the experienced listener.

Sign of the Beaver, by Elizabeth Speare. Speare, an expert on colonial America, tells us the story of a frontier boy left alone to care for the family's cabin. His survival depends on his wits, his courage, and the friendship he makes with the local Native Americans.

OLDER CHILDREN (TWELVE AND UP)

Shadow Spinner, by Susan Fletcher. A girl in the Arabian court helps Shahrazad remember her stories. Lots of close calls and suspense.

December Rose by Leon Garfield. Barnacle, a London chimney sweep, survives by his wits, but learns about family love from an unlikely trio of Thames boaters. Humorous, but full of danger and suspense.

True stories of heroism, such as the series called "Everyday Heroes" in *Reader's Digest* accounts, are great for this age.

Happiness increases in
direct proportion to the
expansion of empathy.

—J. Donald Walters,
Education for Life

CHAPTER FOUR

Learning to Love with
Pets and Pseudo Pets

PEOPLE THE WORLD OVER smile, coo, and reach out to babies and toddlers. Whether it is their innocence, vulnerability, or just plain cuteness, little ones awaken protective, nurturing emotions in adults.

Children, too, naturally respond to anything smaller and more vulnerable than themselves. Watch their reactions to characters such as Paddington Bear, Stuart Little, or Pooh. That opening of the heart is also apparent in the love of children toward animals, especially baby animals. Even the *photo* of a baby animal will evoke such an intense feeling in the heart that children "Ooh" and "Ah" over it.

Nothing stimulates the natural love of a child's heart better than a pet. And if you live in a situation where pets are impossible, don't skip this chapter just yet! Later on I will discuss some substitutes for live animals.

pets

Because our culture motivates boys to be "manly" and not show the softer emotions, pets are especially important as a socially acceptable outlet for boys to show tenderness.

Even older children, who are invested in "being cool," can't help responding to animals. Sandi Goodwin, the fifth and sixth grade teacher in the school where I am director, has a big dog—half Lab, half chow—named Hannah. Sandi and I notice that when she brings Hannah to school with her, the atmosphere in the class changes. Although at these ages the children can be edgy and critical with each other (hormones are having a big effect), when Hannah is there the children are *softer* somehow, less inclined to pick at each other.

In another school where I taught, the first and second grade teacher had a beautiful blonde cocker spaniel named Sarah or, as she was often called, Sarah-Dog. The staff told parents and visitors that we had a dog at school to teach responsibility, to give students a comforting friend who always loved them unconditionally, and to help them learn calmness (when their energy got frenetic, the dog barked, providing instant feedback). These are all good reasons for having a pet in the home or classroom, but the most important reason is that *pets help children develop the heart's capacity to love.*

At that school, I took over a fifth grade class midyear when their teacher had to leave. They had two pet rats in the classroom. I love most animals, but I would never have allowed my class to adopt rats! They reminded me of dungeons and tenements; they gave me the creeps.

But there they were, and I would have been a real meanie if I insisted the children give them away. They took care of the rats, cleaned their cage, and held them—and they begged and begged me to hold them too. The kids often came up to my desk, a rat snuggling or even running around under their clothing (!), and looked at me with puppy eyes, pleading, "They're so sweet; you'd love them if you'd just hold them."

After two months of this, I realized how important it was to them, and I finally gave in. Though I can't say I learned to *love* the rats, holding them was entertaining, and the joy it brought the children was worth it. The class more fully accepted me into their family when I expanded my love to include their pets.

When we started our school in Portland, Oregon, we were in a building where we could not have pets—or at least not furry ones! So we got a young parakeet named Tweety. I worked with Tweety daily during the summer, taming and training him so that he would readily step up onto a child's finger. It was worth the effort.

The first time a first or second grader feels the tiny, delicate parakeet feet resting on his finger, his eyes light up with sheer delight. To keep the bird from flying away, he must be calm and still. The children's interest in the bird's well-being is an important part of the classroom; they vie to feed him and change his water.

The tenderness that a pet creates in children is not a distraction from the curriculum, but part of the curriculum itself in a school or home with a goal of teaching children calm compassion.

stuffies open the heart, too

Another way to encourage the opening of the heart stimulated by live animals is with stuffed animals—or as we call them, stuffies. Children are able to find companionship and unconditional acceptance even from an inanimate animal. My friend Lorna tells me that sometimes when her eight-year-old son is upset, she hears him in his room talking to his stuffed tiger, Stripes.

In a study of 152 preschoolers, psychologist Marjorie Taylor, a professor at the University of Oregon, found that about half of the time preschoolers played with make-believe pals inspired by toys. According to Taylor, "Imaginary friends play an important role in a child's development. What we have shown in previous work is that having an imaginary companion is associated with advanced social understanding—being able to take the perspective of another person."

At the first day of our summer program this year—as I was finishing this book—a kindergartner ran up to me, holding a terra-cotta bird that sits in a flower pot outside her classroom. During the school year, Frannie had often played with the bird, making it "nests" out of grass clippings. Smiling broadly, Frannie said, "Usha, Usha, the little bird remembered me!"

Cute and sweet? Yes, but it is much more. The role-playing and this child's developing ability to see the world from another's perspective are part of her learning to establish relationships with others and relate to their realities.

Bring a Buddy Day is an annual event at our school. Karen, our primary teacher, first created Bring a Buddy Day for her class. Children brought their stuffies to school with them. Karen really played it up: the children had a tea party with chairs for their stuffies, and they all read books aloud to their stuffies. They (children *and* stuffies, presumably) loved it.

And in fact, a surprising result was that the older grades asked, "Why can't *we* have a Buddy Day?" (If we had suggested this first, they probably would have groaned, "That's so baby!") So our next stuffie day was a whole-school Bring a Buddy Day, and boys and girls all the way up through sixth grade showed up with their buddies. At recess I was amazed to see that the primary class boys were playing four-square with their buddies! Each put his stuffie at the corner of his square. As the boys moved around the squares, they moved the little animals along with them. It is rare to see this kind of sweetness combined with active play, especially by boys, who often feel they cannot reveal any softness to their peers.

fairies, elves, and imaginary playmates

The other category of "pseudo pets" is imaginary beings, such as elves and fairies. Most children love the idea of the existence of creatures tinier than they are who have the power of magic. The school's primary class went to see a theater production of *Peter Pan*. One of the mothers took her son's little sister, Evie, who was only three years old. I asked her, "How did you like the play?"

Evie took a deep breath and with wide eyes and a big smile began chattering animatedly. I was surprised, to say the least. Until this moment, Evie had been too shy to talk to me; she had barely been able to acknowledge my greetings. She told me more and more about the production, speaking too fast for me to understand. Suddenly, I knew exactly what had thrilled her so when I caught the words *"Tinker Bell!"*

Karla, a preschool teacher I once worked with at the Living Wisdom School in Nevada City, California, used this enthusiasm for small creatures to create an ongoing adventure for her children. Located in a rural area, the school had three giant cedar trees near the classrooms. Each trunk was so big that it took at least three kindergartners, arms outstretched, to reach around it. In the shade underneath there was a special aura of shelter and protection.

Karla told the children that devas, spirits, and plant fairies came there because they loved the trees as the children did. She suggested the children might like to leave presents for the fairies. Asking for ideas about what the fairies might like encouraged the children to practice seeing another point of view in a way that flowed easily for them.

Together the class decided on treats such as tiny strawberries, tiny cubes of cheese, and useful items such as toothpick logs and spool chairs. The children arranged their gifts on leaves and left them under the cedars. The next morning their gifts were gone and a flower was there with a tiny note saying "Thank you!" This little exchange went on for a month or two and filled the children with love and joy.

Pets, stuffies, or elves and fairies; think of them not merely as child's play but as important opportunities for developing a child's heart-capacity to love. That capacity to love, to tune in to others' realities, is a basis for compassion. The idea of elves and fairies inspires almost all children. However, for the more scientifically minded child—the type who figures out early on who Santa Claus is—pets are more likely to bring the same kind of expansiveness.

The mainstream scientific community has not studied the effects of all of my recommendations for nurturing compassionate children. The importance of pets, however, is endorsed by the American Academy of Child Adolescent Psychology, which says on its website: "Children raised with pets show many benefits. Developing positive feelings about pets can contribute to a child's self-esteem and self-confidence. Positive relationships with pets can aid in the development of trusting relationships with others. A good relationship with a pet can also help in developing non-verbal communication, compassion, and empathy."

If you had a pet as a child, you probably have fond memories of childhood experiences of warmth and love with the animal, but you may not have realized how your relationship with an entity dependent on you for affection and interaction helped to develop your ability to form relationships. You can give that gift to your children too, through having a pet and through recognizing the value of their "imaginary friends."

1. ENTER into your young child's fantasies with his stuffed animals and dolls in a small way. If your child is carrying his stuffie as you leave to go to the store, you might ask, "Does Teddy want to ride to the store with us?" This encourages the child to think about the desires of "someone" outside of himself. Of course, you can do the same with a real pet. (Do this selectively; asking at every opportunity would be intrusive into your child's private relationship.)

2. IF YOUR CHILD wants to bring a doll or stuffie along on trips or to the table for a meal, allow it if at all possible. Don't scoff at your child's treating inanimate objects as real; he is learning to love and to include others in his happiness.

3. WHEN YOUR CHILD FORGETS or puts off feeding her pet or changing the litter, do not nag. Better to just state matter-of-factly that the pet suffers when we forget, then accompany the child to take care of the pet. Most children need more time sharing tasks with parents anyway. Look at it as an opportunity for you to be with your child and to model nurturing.

4. IN MOST CITIES, you can find a Catholic church that holds an annual animal-blessing day, usually associated with St. Francis. If the idea appeals to you, phone some of the churches to find out when it occurs and take your child and pet for the event. You could read a good children's book about St. Francis before you go. I recommend Margaret Hodges' *Brother Francis and the Friendly Beasts* and Francis Colony Elliott's *The Wolf of Gubbio*. (See appendix 3, Recommended Read-Alouds.)

5. LET CHILDREN KNOW you appreciate their empathy. When your child does something thoughtful for his pet—for example, comforting it after a sudden noise—comment on his thoughtfulness and understanding.

6. IF YOUR CHILD BEGS you to rescue or adopt a kitten or puppy but it's just not possible for your family to take it in, you may be tempted to brush aside or discourage her feelings. Instead, support your child's feelings of compassion and validate her open heart. You could agree with her about how appealing the animal is, then gently but firmly explain why you cannot bring it home to live with you.

7. VOLUNTEER at the local animal shelter with your children. Some shelters will not allow minors to help, but together you can collect towels (shelters always need clean towels) and donate them. Or you can call and ask what brand of pet food they use and ask your children if they would like to give a portion of their allowance or birthday money to buy a bag. Some children enjoy this so much that they ask friends for a small donation for the local shelter in lieu of birthday gifts. However, if your child doesn't respond to this suggestion, don't force it. Forcing a child to give when he is not ready will simply make him resent giving.

8. MOST CHILDREN who are encouraged in their heart's natural love of pets will also take an interest in babies. You and your child can volunteer to give a young mother an afternoon off by caring for her infant or toddler. How you nurture and entertain a baby provides a wonderful example for your child, especially your youngest who seldom sees you in this role. Give your child plenty of opportunities to help. He can throw the blankie in the dryer to get it warm, sing songs to the baby, entertain the baby while you change a diaper. Children as young as nine or ten can learn to play with toddlers and entertain them so well that you can virtually be in the background. Plenty of praise for the older child's abilities, and predictions of future success if he decides to be a parent, help him to realize his accomplishments and feel good about giving love to others. (Note: It is important you wait until your child is old enough to be helpful to do this, or he will be jealous of your attention to another child.)

9. IF YOU DO NOT HAVE PETS, care for neighbors' pets while they are on vacation. Young children can go with you and watch what you do and older children can learn what is needed with you helping, until they are able to do it on their own. Many people also like their animals checked on during the day while they are at work.

10.   TAKING ON THE RESPONSIBILITY of keeping a pet calm helps a child learn to control his breath and calm down. Put your child in charge of soothing a pet while in the bath or while waiting at the veterinarian. Teach him how to be soothing—to use a soft voice and loving touch with slow stroking.

11.   READ ALOUD books and stories about animals. There are hundreds to choose from. I especially like (in age appropriate order from six to twelve years) Janell Cannon's *Stellaluna*, Dick King-Smith's *Babe, The Gallant Pig*, Shelia Burnford's *The Incredible Journey*, and Margaret Stanger's *That Quail, Robert*. Details of these and other suggested books are found in appendix 3.

When your thoughts are geared in a positive direction, your feelings are peaceful.

—Richard Carlson,
Don't Sweat the Small Stuff

CHAPTER FIVE

High-Mindedness

RICHARD CARLSON'S STATEMENT sounds so simplistic
that it is easy to miss its significance: when we think positive thoughts, our feelings become peaceful. And its cor-
ollary is important: when our thoughts are negative, we
become edgy, irritable, even angry or agitated.

High-mindedness is the practice of focusing our thoughts
in a positive direction. From countless research studies in
the field of medicine we know that positive thinking aids
healing. For example, people who believe they will get well
from cancer die at a lower rate than those who lack that
confidence. Authors ranging from Norman Cousins back
in the seventies (*Anatomy of an Illness*) to Caroline Myss
more recently (*Anatomy of the Spirit*) have documented the
power of positive thoughts on health. It is time to apply
this knowledge to our child-rearing. Keeping the thoughts
focused on uplifting topics and away from scary news and
images is especially important for children because they
have little experience in filtering out unpleasantness and
violence.

Merely bringing a distasteful element into the conversation can destroy children's calmness and contentment, and they will act it out in different ways. I remember many trips in the school van in my early days of teaching fifth and sixth grades at the first Living Wisdom School. We'd drive down Highway 49 toward Auburn, California, through the Sierra Nevada foothills, passing tall fir forests and then peaceful horse ranches. Unfortunately, I did not understand how to help the children channel their negative energy very well. The kids would be happy to be going somewhere together, chattering and snacking. Then one particular child would begin to tell in gruesome detail the plot of the horror movie he had seen or maybe to describe graphically the rotted dead squirrel we just passed in the road.

Pretty soon the kids would begin poking each other with their elbows and making complaints such as, "Susan, Joe's kicking the back of my seat!" The noise in the van would escalate and the joyful anticipation of the trip would vanish in general rowdiness. These events might seem unrelated to the boy's "low-minded" conversation, but time and time again I have watched a group's harmony disintegrate after an "icky" topic has been introduced.

Perhaps this idea sounds a little far-fetched to you. In the research done by psychologist John Bargh and others on priming (that is, influencing behavior by prior input), we find examples of human behavior influenced even more subtly. In his book *Blink*, Malcolm Gladwell summarizes some of Bargh's studies. In one of two groups of adults, the participants were asked to make sentences out of five word combinations. Each combination in the first group contained a word such as *aggressively, rude,* or *disturb,* and in the second group a word such as *considerate, patiently,* or *respect.* The time the participants took to construct sentences was recorded. They were not told that the real behavior being measured was how long they would wait to interrupt a conversation in order to deliver a note as they left the tester's office. Those in the group primed with the words *aggressively* and so on, interrupted after five minutes, on average. A whopping 82 percent of those in the group primed with the words such as *considerate* never interrupted before the experiment was called off after ten minutes. Many other studies have shown the power of suggestion on behavior, and this knowledge is consistently applied in advertising.

Children are more relaxed and loving if, whenever possible, we keep their attention away from violence and degrading topics. We do not introduce algebra until children have the intellectual capacity to cope with it; similarly, we should not introduce emotionally charged information until they have some emotional maturity. As they mature into puberty and show more curiosity about world events, they have more ability to deal with that knowledge emotionally—you'll find much more about this in chapter 11. (Parents who fear that sheltering their children from the "real world" will make them fragile can find that issue addressed in the chapter 11 section "*Not* Hothouse Flowers.")

Paying attention to the beauty and kindness surrounding us develops sensitivity and gives a calmer outlook on life because it brings our focus to the moment, away from anxiety about the future or past. Francis Hodgson Burnett put it more poetically in *The Secret Garden*:

Where you tend a rose, my lad,
A thistle cannot grow.

Choosing to appreciate the small joys in life helps children (and adults!) to relax and expand their awareness outside of themselves. Parents and teachers can encourage this attitude by their own example and by playing games of positive thinking.

noticing

I observed the joyful energy that focusing on the positive brings in a Palo Alto Living Wisdom classroom, filled with happy, smiling faces. One of my colleague Barbara's teaching activities is a practice she calls *Noticing*. During "Sharing" time first thing each morning, she tells the class about the little joys she's already noticed that day; for example, a flower blooming by the parking lot, the way the clouds look in the sky, or the smile on someone's face. Student volunteers also share something special they have noticed that morning.

Noticing continues throughout the school day. When something beautiful occurs, Barbara calls the class's attention to it: "Children, I *notice* the way the light coming through the window is shining on Shelly's painting." "Boys and girls, let's *notice* the beautiful sounds the rain is making on the windows." "I *notice* that everyone is smiling because they like this story!" When children see something exceptional, they share it with the class and receive acknowledgment for helping everyone else to see it. Sometimes students draw a picture of something wonderful they have noticed.

This attention on uplifting moments helps the children (and the teacher!) be on the lookout for them. Gradually, the children—even those who used to focus on the negative and complain a lot—begin to be happier and more harmonious with each other. Families certainly can do the same thing at home, perhaps in a less formal way. Imagine how much happier we would all be if each day we were *looking* for positive moments.

The concept of Gratitude Journals has been popularized (by Oprah, for one) to the point of being trite, but people are so ardent about them because they are effective. If we want contentment, sincere gratitude is actually a very practical living skill.

I once had a boyfriend who asked me every evening when he came over or called, "What was your most inspiring moment of the day?" As I reflected on the day's events, I would first remember the day's difficulties! Then, as I finally recalled a special moment and began to describe it, a couple more would spring to mind. I realized there were always uplifting events—such as the moment a little girl visiting from Korea put her hand in mine as we walked, or the moment in the parking lot when a student said, "Hey, look at that" and pointed, and all the children stopped their game to admire a rainbow. As my friend and I shared these kinds of episodes day by day, I began to feel a greater sense of peace and flow of grace.

Your family can experience more peace by sharing gratitude moments at dinner every evening. Everyone shares an incident from the day that they are grateful for—an accomplishment, an act of friendship, or anything. At first, this might be difficult for children; they will tend to remember only the previous hour or so! But if given encouragement and reminded of the good things about their day that the parent knows about, they will gradually begin to remember more.

Of course, the most important way to help our children see the good in life is to practice high-mindedness ourselves. "If you are not in the habit of noticing goodness and beauty around you or of sharing those experiences with your children, at first it may seem a bit artificial to do so. But it takes practice to banish old habits and establish new ones," Lorna Knox tells us in *Scary News*. Parents who make a habit of finding fault shouldn't be startled to realize one day that their children whine and complain a lot! And parents who notice and rejoice in life's small blessings often have children who do the same.

violence in the news

In the days and weeks that followed the terrorist attacks of September 11, 2001, much was written about helping children deal with feelings of insecurity, fear, and confusion. The emphasis on allowing children to express their emotions and doubts, and on giving them reassurance was positive. We do need to talk openly and express sorrow and fear to be able to move through or beyond these emotions.

But many adults do not know how to help children with the moving-beyond-it part. Discussions in which children get the chance to process their emotions produce some relief simply because children have had the opportunity to have their feelings accepted. This is good, but if we actually help children move in the direction of positive action or inner peace, that is even better. When we express negative emotions through crying or beating a pillow, we may feel calmer, but it is a purged feeling, passive in a way. When we actually do something positive for ourselves or others—such as exercising intensely or writing letters to firemen—we may experience a more powerful, active inner calm.

As Lorna Knox says, "The headlines and evening news will always show that people are capable of evil, but you will have to show your children that acts of love are even more common. . . ." Teachers and parents should not stop with merely allowing children to express their anxieties about scary news, but should creatively help their children express their high ideals and thus return to the creative, joyful state that is naturally a part of childhood.

During the Gulf War some of the children in the primary class at the Living Wisdom School in Nevada City came to school asking lots of questions about the war. Their parents had been watching and listening to the news. Because these six- and seven-year-old children were hearing media coverage that they were too young to understand, they worried about being bombed or attacked. The violence portrayed on television, especially, had created scary visual images and likely raised the children's stress levels. Parents may not have recognized the low level of anxiety that the children were experiencing, but the children's questions and comments at school alerted their teacher, Toby Moorhouse.

Toby explained to them that they were safe and did everything she could to help them understand intellectually that their homes and families were not at risk. But she felt the need for something that would engage the children's feelings to shift their preoccupation with the news back to awareness of their own lives. To help them, she created a Count Your Blessings bulletin board.

She cut stems out of green paper and put them on the bulletin board. Children helped her cut out flower blossoms from brightly colored paper. Each day anyone who had a blessing to share (a blessing could be as small as seeing a hawk on the way to school or a fun bike ride) could write it on a flower and add it to the beautiful display of blessings on the board. The children eagerly collected positive experiences so they could participate in the display, and their anxieties calmed down. This would be easy to do at home, too. You don't have to use empty stems; you could just cover the refrigerator or a door with "flower blessings." (Or if flowers are too feminine for some, use a cutout that is more appropriate for your family—perhaps the silhouette of a bird flying.)

Years later, after the September 11 attacks, we did a similar thing at our school. Our fourth, fifth, and sixth graders designed world flags to express their hopes for future harmony among all races and nations and religions. They created many beautiful flags that expressed their aspirations for peace; for example, one in which the planet earth floated on the background of the American flag, and another of the planet radiating rainbow colors into the universe. In these ways, we redirect children's attention toward uplifting, creative avenues, model positive action, and practice solution consciousness rather than problem consciousness.

be solution-conscious

When something unfortunate happens, you model to your child a choice: to take it calmly and look for the positive or to let negative emotions take over. When our energy is tied up in disappointment and anger at others, there is little room for giving or loving. If a restaurant order takes too long and comes to the table cold, you can focus on how busy the waiter is and what a hard job he has. Or if it's not busy, and he's simply inept, you can ask calmly for the restaurant to make things right. When we model looking for what we can learn from difficult situations rather than looking to blame others, children will learn the same life skill.

We all know people who are happy and appreciate the good things in their lives—despite disappointment, adversity, and loss. Conversely, we all probably know someone who has many blessings but who sees only difficulties and finds no satisfaction in life. Children are no different: some are full of joy and enthusiasm even though their circumstances are difficult, and others have a gloomy outlook or a tendency to focus on their complaints. It will help your child to be positive if you show confidence that he can cope with unpleasant experiences. When parents treat childhood's minor ups and downs as normal, children learn that they can weather setbacks and disappointments.

It is good to protect your child, but do not overdo it. If parents react to their child's difficulties with more energy than they do to his reports of success and victories, the child learns quickly which gets the parents' attention. He will magnify every little difficulty and begin to see small upsets as bigger than they are. This child may not develop the emotional reserves to give much compassion to others.

Give children as much energy for noticing and sharing their highs as their lows. If children develop the habit of a positive outlook at an early age, they will have a tremendous advantage for leading a happy adult life and including others in their happiness.

1. COLLECT CATALOGS, magazines, travel brochures, and old picture books from the second-hand store. Some rainy, cold weekend, take them all out and announce that you're going to have a "what makes us happy" art project. Cut out the pictures and paste them on a colored poster board. (Hint: If you have lots of pictures of the beach, the forest, animals, and the like, you will have more uplifting collages than if you use toy catalogs!) As you cut and paste, you might share memories from your childhood evoked by the pictures.

2. PRACTICE "NOTICING." If that proves to be difficult for your family, you may need some help forming the habit. To get started, make a "positive comment" jar. Every time someone notices and shares something beautiful or says something good about someone else, put a nickel or dime in the jar. Insincere comments made just to get coins into the jar do not count. You will know the difference, and your children will too. Make it fun to fill up the jar, and when it's full have your children decide on a worthy cause to donate the money to—perhaps the local animal shelter or food bank.

3. EXPLAIN what blessings are and give some examples; let your children talk about the blessings in their lives. Give each child a paper leaf or blossom cutout; have them write their name and a blessing and let them tack it on a bulletin board, paste it on a poster board, or affix it to the refrigerator door. Whenever a blessing appears (an unexpected visit from a special friend, a rainbow, anything at all), talk about it and put up a new blossom or leaf with the blessing written or drawn on it.

4. ENCOURAGE high-mindedness by surrounding yourself and your child with beauty and meaningful objects. Set up a nature table in a hallway or entry where you can display your finds from nature walks, or gems and minerals, or one of your child's precious collections. The display will not grow stale if you let your child select the objects, arrange them, and change the arrangement seasonally.

5. TO KEEP your child's thoughts uplifted, avoid violent video games and movies with intense, adult emotional content. (See more about this topic in chapter 11.)

6. PLAN some suggestions that you can make to help your child move toward higher thoughts of protecting or saving others the next time he acts out "violence" fantasies.

7. ENJOY TOYS AND BOOKS that encourage imagination, creative play, problem solving, and cooperation. (See appendices 3 and 4 for suggestions.)

8. TO HELP your children be high-minded, be very selective of the peers with whom they associate. (More about this, too, in chapter 11.)

9. IF YOUR CHILD COMPLAINS about his day, listen carefully to his frustration and empathize, reflecting his feelings. "You must have felt disappointed" (or "sad" or "upset"). But after he has finished, help him to remember a positive aspect of the day with a thoughtful question, such as, "What did you do in art today?" or "Did you see your friend Jamey at lunch?"

10.   HELP CHILDREN TO CREATE positive language skills. Find new ways to uplift one another with words. Make a game of using a new positive word every day. Our language is rich with words like *bountiful* and *gracious* that help us express the higher side of life.

11.   WHEN YOU put your child to bed, lie down beside her and ask her to share the best or most inspiring moment of her day. Then share yours. Or you begin and then let her tell you hers. Make this a daily practice, and you will see great change in your contentment and the intimacy of your relationship.

Part Two

Calming Body and Mind

THE GOAL OF PART TWO is to help you and your child slow down, still the mind, and create space for both calmness and creativity. *Slowing down* means the willingness to wait and see what unfolds. *Stilling the mind* creates a possibility for something special to occur without having expectations that things will go a certain way. When we are caught up in our own self-centered desires and emotions, we cannot perceive subtleties in our environment; in calmness we can access our intuition.

If you have been using some of the suggestions in Part One with mixed results, you might skip over this section for now and read chapters 11 and 12 on environment and adults. You may find that characteristics either in your child's environment or in yourself are making it difficult for your child to relax and respond to your efforts. Once you are able to calm yourself and the outside influences on your child, you will see great changes for the better. Then you may come back to the ideas in Parts One and Two and find that experimenting with them flows more easily.

If there is one chapter of the first ten that I would recommend to *every* parent, it's chapter 6, on music. If you honestly use the practical suggestions about music in chapter 6, without inserting the prejudice of your own likes and dislikes for different music genres, I believe you will see changes in your children's behavior quickly, especially in children young enough not to have developed definite musical "tastes."

Music [is] a universal language.
It isn't just a matter of taste—
there's music that lifts your
consciousness and music that
debases it. It's not necessary
for music always to be calm or
tranquil, but in the end it needs
to uplift and take you to a higher
state of consciousness.

—J. Donald Walters

CHAPTER SIX

Music to Soothe

WHEN I WAS JUST TWENTY-TWO and living in Atlanta, I was a member of the staff who cared for twenty-five children in their "cottage" at the Georgia Retardation Center. When the professional staff was absent on the weekends, the younger staff and I relaxed and tossed out the usual routine. First thing on Saturday morning, we would change the elevator music piped through the building to our favorite rock music station. By lunchtime the children would be "bouncing off the walls," so much so that it was hard to get them seated and calmed down enough to eat. If we hoped to have any peace during the meal, we learned to turn off the rock music about a half-hour before lunch.

It was a few years later that I learned music could be used for the opposite effect—to calm and center children whose energy is out of control or children who are having trouble focusing. In 1980, one of my graduate school professors told me about Steven Halpern, whose new-age music, he said, was too relaxing to listen to while driving! That sounded far-fetched, but intriguing. Years later, my yoga teacher, who used music to help us relax in class, mentioned that music affects us much more than words because we are really just vibrations—all matter being energy—and music is vibration too. This made sense to me, and I started thinking about using music in my classroom, not just for ambiance, but more consciously to help children to concentrate and even to solve problems. But first, I had an opportunity to try it at home.

My teenage stepson was packed and ready to go to the airport. He had spent the summer with us in the California foothills, working part-time for a neighbor and getting acquainted with our West Coast friends. Now it was time to go back to Georgia. He is an enthusiastic, vivacious person, but I had never seen him this keyed up. He was pacing back and forth from the kitchen to the living room, unaware that he was talking nonstop. Perhaps the nervousness and anxiety about his flight wasn't only because of the trip and anticipation of seeing his friends, but also a way to disguise some regret in leaving. I would sometimes give him a shoulder massage to help him relax, but now he was too agitated to be still even for five minutes.

His dad quietly said to me, "I don't know what will happen when he has to sit in the car for an hour and a half."

Then I remembered what I had been learning about the effects of music. I found a calming CD, put it in the player, turned it up, and whispered to my husband, "Let's see if this has any effect."

The change in Patrick was astounding. Within five or six minutes he was sitting on the couch chatting with his dad,

calm and compassionate children

not relaxed but with enough anxiety released that he could sit down and be coherent. I could not believe how quickly his energy had changed. This was my first experience of using music consciously to help someone calm down. Here was an incredible tool for working with children, and I had not been using it!

After seeing the rapid change in my stepson when I intentionally played music to soothe him, I began to use music more consciously in the classroom. I had played Mozart during silent math periods to help children concentrate, but the first time I used music to help calm my class was one afternoon after lunch recess. The ten- and eleven-year-olds burst into the classroom agitated. Their faces were red; they were all talking at once, trying to tell me about a dispute they had had with a few children from another class. There was no way I could go on with the lesson plan with them in this state. They would not learn anything.

"Okay. I can't hear with you all talking at once. We'll talk about it, but first I want you to get a glass of water, sit down, and keep silent for five minutes while you drink and relax."

I put on the album *Secrets of Love* (see appendix 4). After just a few bars of the music, the atmosphere in the classroom started to change. The students' jerky movements and agitated expressions relaxed. Tension visibly drained out of them. Even though this was what I had hoped would happen, I was amazed at how fast and apparent the changes were. At the end of five minutes I turned the music down and asked who would like to talk about the issue. Only three hands went up.

Other children said, "Oh, let's not; let's just work on our projects." It ended up that only two students, those directly involved, needed to resolve things with me verbally. The harmony and flow of the music had enabled the others to let go of the negative emotions they had gotten caught up in. Music can help children relax after all sorts of minor and major crises.

physiological effects of music

Research on the power of music to affect organic systems has been extensive. Experiments in the seventies and eighties showed that plants grew better "listening" to Bach and Indian classical ragas than to rock music, and that cows who heard classical music gave more milk. Since then, numerous studies have been done on the physiological effects of music on the human body.

Two cycling objects—whether living cells or inanimate objects such as pendulum clocks—when brought near each other will adopt the same rhythm. This process is called *entrainment*—the overriding of an internal rhythm such as heartbeat by an external pulse or beat. Similarly, we've learned that music has a direct effect on the respiratory rate, the heart rate, and systolic blood pressure. Our brain waves, heart rhythms, respiration, and emotions change depending on the rhythm of the music we are listening to.

Entrainment can happen even with vibrations we are not aware of. We are so sensitive to the vibrations around us that we become attuned to the acoustic oscillations of the electrical currents we live with. Dr. Carla Hannaford reports that in her workshops in Canada and the United States, people can easily match the pitch of B natural because it aligns with the 60-cycles-per-second electrical system that is the standard in these countries. In Europe, however, where the standard is 50 cycles per second, people can easily match a G sharp note (which aligns with 50 cycles), but struggle with trying to hit a B note.

We know that fear, anxiety, and stress raise the heartbeat and respiratory rate. Due to the process of entrainment, music with a fast tempo can do the same thing. In fact, such music can even make the heartbeat *incoherent*. (*Incoherence* means lacking in order and efficient functioning.) According to Dr. Hannaford, in *Awakening the Child Heart,* "incoherent heartbeat and breath rate are also characteristic of orphaned monkeys and children," who for obvious reasons live in a state of stress and fear. That certain forms of music have a similar effect on the body is a measure of the negative power that music can wield.

brain waves and learning

In addition to calming an agitated child, the process of entrainment can also be used to bring about coherence of the breath and heartbeat, enhancing learning. The normal resting heartbeat has a wide range of normal, 60 to 100 beats per minute in adults and 75 to 120 in school-age children. The heart rate speeds up not only with exercise, but also with stress, fear, and anxiety. There is much in the environment that causes children anxiety (see chapter 11). When we are in a calm and focused state, our hearts have a slow, steady beat.

Listening to music with a steady rhythm of around 60 beats per minute helps slow the heart rate to a calm measured pace and also slows the breathing. As the breath and heart rate become slower and more regular, the agitated mind calms too, as brain waves slow from the usual beta waves cycling from 14 to 30 hertz—or more—to alpha waves, cycling from 8 to 13 hertz.

Alpha is the state that very young children's brains are in most of the time. Watch a two-year-old child walking down the street hand in hand with an adult; you will see the adult moving purposefully, probably thinking of the future—where he's going and what he will be doing—while the child dawdles, fully absorbing the experience, noticing a weed in the sidewalk crack or an ant. That state of absorption in the moment, rather than in stressing about the past or future, is an optimal learning state. (According to some, even more interesting is the theta state, in which the brain cycles from 4 to 8 hertz—the usual rate of infants when awake. The transition point between theta and alpha, around 7.5 hertz, is said to bring the most clarity and peace of mind.)

As the child grows older and the beta state becomes more prominent, she can still access the calm alpha state if she is not stressed or overstimulated, and if her parents and teachers know how to help her go back to that state, especially through music. Slow selections of baroque music, Gregorian chant, and other music with the 60-beats-per-minute rhythm will produce this effect. Baroque music, perhaps because of its highly organized and structured nature, also increases mental clarity and memory. (Baroque music was created during the sixteenth, seventeenth, and early eighteenth centuries; well-known baroque composers include Bach, Vivaldi, and Handel. Baroque music gave rise to the sonata and concerto forms later used by Mozart, whose music also contains repetitive, strong underlying patterns.)

The fact that baroque and other slow-beat music enhances learning has been touted for decades. Georgi Lozanov, a Bulgarian psychiatrist, developed methods on which later techniques known as Superlearning and Accelerated Learning were based. These methods use certain types of music to increase brain processing speed and retention. More recently, researchers have claimed that math and spatial intelligence are increased by listening to Mozart, and Don Campbell even trademarked the phrase *the Mozart Effect* to describe the broader phenomenon of "the transformational powers of music in health, education, and well-being." He and other educators sell CDs especially for the purpose of increasing focus and learning. Trina Gardner, Living Wisdom's preschool teacher, says when she plays calming music with an even tempo, "Even the children who prefer physical activity will work on a project twice as long."

Because our traditional education is biased toward mental development, the emphasis on the positive effects of music on children has focused on intellectual progress (for example, the higher math scores of children who study music). What has not been as widely discussed are the other, psychological benefits that 60-beats-per-minute, highly organized music produces: calmness, inner peace, and the ability to control one's impulses. These traits are exactly what our children need to develop—or retain —if we want them to be compassionate.

The power of music to influence behavior is recognized in fields other than education, including business and healing. It is a comment on our culture that research on the effects of music and consumers has been implemented more widely than research on music and children. Businesses use music both to increase worker productivity and to increase consumer buying. The music playing in the aisles of your favorite chain store is no accident (unless the employees have subverted the system, as we did at the retardation home); it is chosen because marketing studies have proven that shoppers buy more when it is playing.

Using music in surgery prep to aid in healing and to relieve pain and anxiety is becoming more and more common. A new practice is rapidly becoming popular: playing the harp for those who are dying. Patients find the music calming, and it eases their stress.

calming music

Teachers and parents do not take full advantage of music's usefulness in relaxing children. Because of media coverage of the Mozart phenomenon, parents have become interested in classical CDs and music lessons for their children for the purpose of increasing math achievement and intellectual development. However, parents and educators could use music in many more ways, to help children

- Calm down when they are overstimulated, angry, or upset
- Cope with stress
- Move through transitions
- Go to sleep

Just as you may give your children vitamins or organic foods to increase their physical health, you can give them music (and silence) to increase their physical, emotional, and spiritual health.

Many more studies need to be done on the positive effects of music on children. However, you really do not need science to tell you what your own observations can show you. The first of this chapter's practical steps will guide you in learning more.

CALMING EXAMPLES

These are examples of selections you can use to calm children when they are overexcited, help them concentrate when they need to focus, and get them to relax when they are fearful or unable to sleep.

- *Secrets of Love* by Donald Walters
- *Relax: Meditations for Flute and Cello* by Donald Walters
- *Music for Accelerated Learning* by Steven Halpern
- *Music for Concentration* by the Arcangelos Chamber Ensemble

Songs you can sing:

• Most lullabies
• "Kumbaya"
• "Michael, Row the Boat Ashore"
• "We Shall Overcome"
• "Silent Night"

using music as an energizer

Of course, you do not want children always to be still. Sometimes you want them to be energetic and active—for example, when you are cleaning up or getting ready to leave the house or classroom. Just as music can be used to calm and soothe, it can be used to activate. Music with a faster beat can help children who are in unwilling or lethargic moods to get moving.

Not all activating music choices are equal, however. Many types of music stimulate children to action and movement, but is their activity purposeful and under control or random and restless? When it's the latter, children fall, knock things over, crash into other children, or have other accidents because their brain waves, heart rate, and respiration are not coherent. Activity and movement can be either calmly focused or wild and out of control. You want to choose activating music that uplifts the energy—not music that makes the child's energy frenetic.

The following examples are energizing to the human body. Unlike some fast-paced music, they uplift the energy without creating a driving energy that stimulates the need for ego-satisfaction. Think of the difference between a child who is unable to focus and whose activity is aimless and agitated, and a child who is cheerful and active—enjoying his activity. You want to find activating music that produces the latter!

- Most Sousa marches, polkas, some Andean music
- Bach's Brandenburg concertos, the allegro movements
- *Medicine Woman* by Medwyn Goodall

Songs you can sing:

- "She'll Be Comin' Round the Mountain"
- "If You're Happy and You Know It"
- "When the Saints Go Marchin' In"
- "Do-Re-Mi" (from *The Sound of Music*)
- "Jingle Bells"

your words are not enough

Reasonable requests are often not enough to calm children down. Although rewards and threats may work for a while, eventually overstimulated children's restless energy will flow out somewhere you may not see—for example, in the classroom, in sleeplessness, or in cruelty to a younger sibling. Children need to *feel* calmness to get control of their energy. *Nonverbal* experiences such as touch, movement, nature, and *music* are effective—perhaps with a few explanatory words—to help children become calmer in the heart both literally and figuratively. You will begin to realize the power of music to help you and your children relax and feel balanced when you do some of the experiments that follow.

calm and compassionate children

First, tune in. Select two samples of music from the calming and activating groups, plus two from what you usually play. Each evening when your children get home from school or when you get home from work, put on one of the selections. As you prepare dinner or relax, observe your children. Don't tell your children what you are doing; just do it! If they know you are experimenting with the effects of music, older children can and will change the outcome. As you observe the effects of different types of music, be sure to observe behavior, rather than your or their likes and dislikes. Children may say, "Oh, you're not going to play that again, are you?" and yet exhibit calm, centered behavior while it is playing.

As you play each type of music, take note of all these ways in which your children respond:

- *Physical reactions*—are their movements controlled or chaotic? Do they gracefully experiment with movement and their bodies, or do they fall, bump into things, or flail about?
- *Voice tone and speed of talking*—Are their voices pleasant or unpleasant to listen to? Are they able to articulate an idea?
- *Listening ability*—When needed, can they focus on what you say, or do they have trouble concentrating?
- *Awareness of realities outside themselves*—Does the music influence their consideration for pets or family members? Do their interactions with others become more or less harmonious?
- *After-effects*—When you turn off the music, what is their demeanor and behavior for the next ten or fifteen minutes?

Making these observations of your children's behaviors will help you to perceive which types of music are helpful for your family.

1. WHEN your child is having trouble with homework, before you help, start one of the calming music selections. Tune in to the rhythm of the music yourself, allowing your voice tone and pace to be calm and reassuring to your child.

2. WHEN your child is lagging and you need her to help pick up her toys or get ready to go, play the activating music you've identified to help increase her controlled physical energy. This music will help *you* get going, too!

3. WHEN your child has trouble going to sleep, give him a warm bath or a foot rub (see chapter 8) while you play a selection from the calming list. Leave it on after you tuck in your child. Not only will this help him relax, but going to sleep with this type of music may also decrease nightmares.

4. BE SURE to keep several selections of calming music in your car. On long trips, they can be invaluable to help your family arrive with a minimum of fuss!

5. WHEN your children squabble, or when a friend is over to play and suddenly the energy goes sour and they are unable to get along, call a refreshment break. Put on one of the music selections you identified for increasing harmony while you chat with them and prepare a special drink, such as warm herbal tea in the winter or sparkling water in the summer. This infusion of uplifting energy—from you, the music, and the drink—will usually be enough to help children lift their consciousness and

solve the problem they were having. Often, the problem will just disappear, and they'll find something new to do.

6. BECOME AWARE of how the music in films affects you and your children. Notice how the changes in heartbeat, breath, adrenaline, and mood are achieved simply through the musical score. Point this out to your children when appropriate, without ruining the movie—for example, when you're watching an old favorite for the second or third time!

7. SET AN EXAMPLE: When you sit down to relax with a cup of tea, play your favorite calming music. When you balance your checkbook or work on paperwork, play slow-tempo baroque music for clarity of mind. Breathe slowly and be conscious of the effects of the music's vibrations on your own body and feelings.

I am absorbed in the magic
of movement and light.
Movement never lies.

—Martha Graham

CHAPTER SEVEN

Movement, Breath, and Touch

CARL, A FIFTH GRADE STUDENT at our school, had so much physical energy that he could not keep himself on task. With good intentions he would start desk work such as writing. A few minutes later he would be out of his seat, sharpening an already sharp pencil and using it to poke someone on the way back to his desk. Finally he would sit down, look at his paper a second or two, and then start tapping his pencil and wiggling a foot. I would catch his eye and ask, "Carl, do you need to run?" Almost always he would say yes with relief and willingly go outside and run twice around the building. He knew from experience that he would have more self-control after some exercise. Three or four minutes later he would be back, refreshed and able to focus for fifteen or twenty minutes.

When Carl started fidgeting again, I would know it was time to give *everyone* a movement break. Students like Carl are often the classroom barometer that lets us know when all the children are in need of movement. Quite often when children are having trouble being still and concentrating, they just need to move—to exert some physical energy. It's as if their bodies are filling with the need to move, and about every hour or so (more often for children younger than seven), the physical energy glass fills up and starts to run over. Getting the children up and doing something active pours some of the energy out of the glass and helps them integrate mind and body. Then they can come back to stillness until the glass refills again.

children need outlets for physical energy

The human body is designed to move. For survival, it is programmed to run (after prey), to crouch and crawl and hide (from predators), to jump (over streams and other obstacles), to throw (spears), and to dig (roots). An incredible amount of activity and physical exertion is needed for the child's body to develop to its potential. Daily exercise is vital for children to achieve the state of calm stillness. Think of exercise as the inhalation and calm stillness as the exhalation: you cannot have one without the other. Lots of movement is *essential* for a child's emotional health and physical and mental calmness.

Some parents think having their children play on sports teams meets that need. However, a couple of practices and a game a week cannot take the place of daily physical challenge and stimulation. In fact, most children need movement hourly!

Some children may *prefer* quiet activities, such as games of pretend or building with a LEGO set; however, regard-

calm and compassionate children

less of their temperaments, all children *need* physical play and movement. Children who do not like sports still need to run, swing, jump, and challenge themselves. Otherwise, they won't develop good balance or a good concept of where their bodies are in space, not to mention cardiovascular fitness. Keeping the body moving is essential not only for children's physical health, but also for their emotional health and physical and mental calmness.

Thirty or forty years ago, we assumed that children's inherent need for physical stimulation and development was satisfied by play alone. That may have been true then, but now children spend so many hours glued to computer or TV screens that they spend much less time in physical play. Not only do they spend less time outdoors, but they also have fewer chances to be physically daring once they're out there—just another reason for them to stay on the couch.

In our modern lawsuit-crazy environment, many activities that are good for children's bodies, such as playground merry-go-rounds, are being eliminated. At the Nevada City Living Wisdom School, a teacher suspended wonderful rope swings from oak trees around the campus, mostly on hillsides. The ropes enabled children to spin and swing in great arcs that went thrillingly high. Sometimes a visitor wondered whether we worried about the danger of falling; in fact, one of our students did slip and break her wrist. On the other hand, in the Portland Living Wisdom School, a student who was quite athletic and poised merely tripped over a hula hoop lying on the ground and broke his arm! Thank goodness both sets of parents were realistic about the bumps, scrapes, and even occasional broken bones that are part of a normal childhood.

When adults think they are protecting their children by exposing them to only "safe" environments, they're usually not considering the long-term results of those restrictions. One benefit of the rope swings, in particular, is the stimulation of children's inner-ear vestibular systems. In children, the fluid in the semicircular canals has not yet thickened. Remember how as a child you loved having an adult pick you up by the hands and swing you around in a circle? You never got as dizzy as the adult would because of the fluidity of your vestibular system. Swinging and spinning stimulate the vestibular system's development, which contributes to body awareness, balance, and grace.

In a completely safe and sanitized world, children would not test their limits or develop their potential—not to mention that they wouldn't have the fun and movement that helps them settle down to mental or creative activity.

movement breaks

Giving children enough opportunities to move will help them enormously with their self-control—the ability to restrain impulses rather than speaking or acting hastily in reactivity. Many of the concepts in this book will help children have self-control, especially the ideas in this chapter and the chapters on music, silence, and environment. However, teaching children self-discipline and control on a basic level is outside the scope of this book. For parents who seek advice in this area, I recommend Becky Bailey's *Easy to Love, Difficult to Discipline* (see appendix 4). Another level of self-control is the capacity to keep busy with worthwhile activities and thoughts and to avoid harmful ones. This type of self-control is addressed in chapters 5 and 10.

Experts say that as a general rule children can sit still and absorb new information for a period of minutes about equal to their years of age. That's right, only ten minutes for the average ten-year-old! Beyond that stretch of time, the child's brain is on overload and needs to work with the material just presented or have some other change of pace. How much longer they can comfortably be still and listen depends on their motivation and on whether they are given something to do with the new information. If they are not engaged and attentive, their energy will leave the brain, go into the muscles, and need release. Kids will tap a pencil, poke a neighbor, wiggle in their chairs. A brief movement break will answer that need and, moreover, oxygenate the blood and enable children to think more clearly.

Too often when children are restless, we are tempted to admonish them, "Sit still. Listen to this"; or we ignore their bodies' needs and let them fidget. How much better if we recognize the need for movement and provide a movement break! Both teachers and parents can use these breaks to help children stay calm and collected. To be calming, a movement break requires some concentration and focus. You can start with activities that require mild exertion and then proceed to one or two requiring mind and body to work together. (All-out exertion can itself be stimulating and make it difficult to bring the children back to focus; save that for longer breaks of at least a quarter-hour.)

To make it fun and to motivate your child to participate, do the movements too, or have your spouse join in. Movement breaks are great when your child is whining and becoming "tired" while doing homework or when you stop on a car trip. Simply say, "Let's take a five-minute play break!" and begin. Put enthusiasm in your voice and move along with the kids. Try this one, for example:

Okay, let's see how fast you can clap your hands fifteen times!
Great! Now run in place as fast as you can for twenty steps.
Reach up to the ceiling as high as you can.
Stretch your arms out to the sides as far as you can reach.
Rub your stomach and pat your head at the same time.
Put your right hand on your left knee and your left hand on
* your right ear.*
Do the opposite.
Both hands on your hips! Take a deep breath and let it out
* slowly but so we can hear it.*
Smile.

When the children in my classes seemed restless or when it was raining too hard to go outside for recess, I often led them in a game of Run Around Chairs. This activity, taught to me by Education for Life teacher Peter MacDow, is a delightful way to give kids aerobic exercise. We shoved the desks and chairs into the middle of the room to make a "track" as large as possible. Then I rehearsed the kids, having them walk clockwise around the track, jog, take baby steps, take giant steps, march, skip, twirl, and crawl. Next we would walk again and review directions: "Forward!" "Reverse!" (turn around and go the opposite direction) and "Backward!" (face the same direction, but go backward).

Lively music gets it going. Bluegrass, Sousa marches, polkas, and some children's music work well. Shouting out lots of movement commands keeps the kids alert and makes it great fun. Watch the children's faces. Soon they will all be smiling and laughing. Try this experiment with just about any group and you will find the same thing. The body likes to have fun moving, and the smiles will come involuntarily.

To keep the activity from getting out of hand, you may have to make a rule that anyone who passes or runs into someone else's back sits out for a minute. Like drivers, children should keep enough distance between them so they can stop if the person in front of them slows down. As the children get the hang of it, you can switch instructions quickly: "Backward! Forward! Reverse! Reverse again!" I usually stand by the CD player to turn the volume down to give the directions, but if you have just one or two children, you will want to join in the running, too. You can do this at home around the dining room table. If it gets too rowdy, turn the music off and play without it.

Run Around Chairs, like similar movement games, has great benefits; it

- Allows children to release some of their physical energy
- Stimulates different parts of the brain than mental activity does

- Helps children focus and settle down to quieter activity

Because the game involves mental concentration—they must really listen and think so as not to confuse "Backward!" and "Reverse!"—they must stay focused and controlled even as they are intensely active. Finally, this kind of physical activity is just plain fun! Give children structured—not chaotic—activity, and they will be more cooperative and eager to work with you.

When movement breaks are not possible—for example, during a religious service or a play or musical performance— you can provide the means for a child's body to get engaged while sitting relatively still. Bring along some Silly Putty or PLAY-DOH to give the child when he becomes restless, and let him play with that. An older child can play with a small puzzle, such as a four by four with fifteen tiles to put into a pattern. The restless physical energy will flow through the movement of the hands and help children stay still.

movements can enhance meaning

All movement is not created equal! Some movements can better help a child reach a state of calmness than others. People describe negativity and depression with words that connote a downward movement of energy, such as *downcast*, *down in the dumps*, *feeling low*, and *having a sinking feeling*. And when we feel joy or enthusiasm, we say we are *uplifted*, *on cloud nine*, *walking on air*, *on a natural high*. This language describes universal experiences. It is unlikely that a person in *any* culture would describe a state of joy and benevolence with a corresponding sinking sensation. Nor could anyone who is depressed, discouraged, or hopeless claim feelings of rising energy.

How does this information assist you in helping children to be happier and more harmonious? Let's say you are doing a few calisthenics. You touch toes, march in place, and do a few sit-ups. Don't stop there. Do some movements that will bring the energy upward in the body, especially to the heart center. Arm movements such as reaching up, imitating rope climbing, clapping, arms out to the side and rotating in circles, and snapping fingers high over the head, will help children bring their energy upward. Then, to get more energy to the brain, do a few eye exercises or a scalp massage. Try exercising both ways—*with* and *without* ending with the upward arm movements—and see if you can tell a difference in both yourself and the children.

Imagine movements you might use to express uplifted feelings, such as love, aspiration, and generosity. For respect and reverence, we put the hands together in front of the heart; for generosity, perhaps hands on the heart and then arms opening outward. For inspiration or aspiration, we might lift our arms toward the heavens.

In preschool, we use a little rhyme, "My Heart Can Pray," with appropriate pointing gestures to the different body parts. The movements are fun, help the very young learn their body parts, and bring the awareness from self outward. I found this anonymous verse in an anthology and added the last verse so children end with gestures that express inspiration. If you don't care for the concept of angels, you might change the last verse to read, "And when I feel/The sunshine's ray/My heart can sing/What words can't say."

Lyrics	Movements
My eyes can see.	*Touch near outside corners of eyes.*
My mouth can talk.	*Touch corners of mouth.*
My ears can hear.	*Touch ears.*
My feet can walk.	*Lift one foot, then the other.*
My nose can smell.	*Point to nose.*
My teeth can bite.	*Point to teeth.*
My lids can flutter.	*Flutter eyelids.*
My hands can write.	*Pretend to write.*
My elbow can bend.	*Bring hands to shoulders.*
My eye can wink.	*Wink one eye, then the other.*
My knee can lift.	*Raise knee and touch with the opposite hand.*
My mind can think.	*Point to forehead.*
And when I feel	*Hands over heart.*
An angel's ray,	*Arms raised in a V-shape.*
My soul can sing.	*Touch heart; extend arms outward.*
My heart can pray.	*Palms together at the heart.*

Notice how the semantic change in the last verse ("and when I feel") slows the rhythm, bringing a change of feeling from action to quiet awareness. You can do this even

calm and compassionate children

with a baby who isn't walking yet. Recite the poem and do the motions, and by age two the toddler will be doing it with you.

If you have ever seen any men's dancing of the South Seas islands, you know that movement can also express strength, energy, and willpower. Marching in place is one movement that expresses these attributes. The following song and its movements express courage and determination. Sing it to the tune of the chorus of the "Battle Hymn of the Republic," the part that begins, "Glory, glory, hallelujah."

I am brave, and I am strong.
I'm courageous all life long.
I can go the extra mile,
Undefeated in every trial.

Motions: After the children learn the words, add these motions, line by line:

Line 1: *Interlace fingers and press palms together at navel; at the same time, bend elbows and tense biceps.*
Line 2: *March in place, lifting knees high.*
Line 3: *Continue marching in place.*
Line 4: *Arms up in a V-shape (on undefeated), then extended out to the sides.*

You can add uplifting gestures to songs and rhymes you already know. By making the words, music, and actions all harmonize together for the feeling you want, you will become more aware of the nuances of the effects of movement, rhythm, and music on both you and your child.

breath and body work

Breath is also a type of movement; healthy breathing expands the lungs and diaphragm. I first learned of the concept of using the breath to calm the mind and emotions when I started doing yoga with Lilias Folan back in the seventies. Now frequent articles in many magazines recommend deep breathing to help manage stress. If you can get an upset child to slow her breathing, her heart rate follows, and the emotions calm down too.

Tanya, a parent of three children who attend my school, described breathing with her daughter Evie, her youngest child. She told our parenting group that when Evie gets over-excited, she helps her calm down by asking her to breathe deeply and by breathing with her. As a toddler, Evie often got into bed with Tanya and her husband. Tanya would hold her close and practice deep breathing very audibly. Before long, Evie would breathe the same way and become still.

"Now that she is almost four, she will often willingly breathe deeply when I ask her to. It is natural for her," Tanya said. "My older children, in contrast, will resist when I ask them to stop and breathe because I did not model this skill when they were very small."

When your young child is upset, remind him to breathe. If you try to talk about the problem while he is still holding his breath, or breathing in short shallow spurts, you are expecting too much. He cannot listen when his whole body is in "fight or flight" mode. Hold him against your chest and take audible long, slow breaths until his breathing starts to calm down to match yours.

calm and compassionate children

Trina Gardner routinely teaches her class to be aware of their breath as a preschool skill-for-living! For example, before the children cross the street, she has them stop, take a deep breath, and let it out slowly. This calms them. If they are excited, it brings them back to awareness of their situation and makes them more attentive to the teacher and traffic. If someone has trouble taking slow breaths, she asks them to "Find your hair. Touch your knee," bringing them back to body awareness before trying again.

touch and water

It is common knowledge that babies who are not held and cuddled fail to thrive even though their other physical needs are met. Physical touch is supportive and calming when done with loving intention. In my school, teachers are encouraged to pat children on the back, hold their hands, or touch them on the shoulder when they are struggling with their work or their emotions. Often, words are not even necessary. When you put your hand on a child's arm and give a loving squeeze and warm smile, it often gives the child the strength to let go of an emotional attachment or to deal with a situation on his own.

Massage is a great tool for calming children. One night when my stepdaughter was about nine, she complained that she could not fall asleep. I sat down on the edge of the bed to talk to her and began to massage her feet, especially using my thumb to stimulate the acupressure points on her soles, and then using long, slow strokes to calm her. As I rubbed her feet we talked, but I also consciously took long, slow breaths and visualized calmness flowing through my hands into her. She found it so relaxing that she began asking me for a foot massage at bedtime. Some children love to have their backs stroked as well. The combination of physical touch and your loving attention gives the space needed for the child to let go of tension and relax into love and peace.

Another calming tactile experience is water on the skin. Did you ever see a child who didn't love to run and play through the spray from a sprinkler? Recently I saw my ten-year-old neighbor walking through my yard. A sprinkler that goes down to the left, up, and then down to the right was watering the garden. Ryan stopped and looked in every direction, obviously checking to see whether he was being watched. Curious about what he was up to, I waited by the window to see. Suddenly, he started trying to outrun the sprinkler. He would wait until it was overhead and then run as fast as he could crosswise in the direction in which the sprinkler was headed—trying to beat it before the water landed on his back. He ran back and forth, laughing and playing this game with the sprinkler for at least a quarter of an hour. I suppose he looked around first because he didn't want to be observed being so "uncool" as to play with a sprinkler, but as soon as he got wet the first time, he completely forgot himself and played with wild abandon.

Water is refreshing. You may not have a sprinkler in your yard, but a bathroom shower will produce a similar effect. The effect of water on the body, and therefore on one's energy, is almost as great as that of music! Children who will play a game for only fifteen minutes or so before becoming bored will beg to stay in the swimming pool after their skin is shriveled and their lips blue. Cold water is activating; warm water is calming. Baths can be just the thing to help children unwind and relax back into themselves. Most children like hot tubs, too.

A parent invited a small class of five- to seven-year-olds to her house a few miles out in the country on a spring day. Although it was late spring, the weather was cloudy and cool. We explored, petted horses, did a craft project, and ate, but the hot tub was the most popular activity. We changed into bathing suits and got in; I expected the children to last about five minutes just sitting in water. But they talked for a long time. They bopped in and out, giggling and enjoying the sensation of cool air, then hot water. Their little bodies were slippery and warm and their spirits were joyful. The hot tub did not calm them in the way a foot rub might (that's a good idea, too, while they are in the water!), but they seemed to come back into their center of joy when they spent time in the hot water. The colder it is outside, the better!

Finally, children need plenty of water *internally* to be at their best. Water is essential for maximizing the electrical transmissions that make up our brain activity. Children who have been out on a hot playground and then have returned inside and not properly rehydrated themselves will actually look dazed. They cannot respond appropriately to intellectual or emotional stimuli. All family members should have their own water bottles when away from the house for more than a half-hour; children will drink water if you are drinking it too.

PRACTICAL STEPS

1. RELEASE your expectations that children should be able to be still for long periods. They are made to move.

2. USE MOMENTS while you are waiting (in line at the post office, for the toast to pop up, or in the car to pick up an older sibling after school) to engage your child in purposeful movement. Cross crawl—touching hands to the *opposite* knees—helps to integrate the right and left sides of the brain. Or make up a pattern of clapping hands together. First both hands, then right, then left, then both is a basic pattern for a young child. Count how many times you can do it without a mistake; when it becomes easy for your child, make up harder patterns. A whining or restless child will focus and engage for a movement game unless utterly exhausted.

3. AT HOME, push the furniture against the wall, put on lively music (such as bluegrass, polkas, the allegro movements of Bach's Brandenburg concertos), and dance with your children. You don't have to know how to dance—think of it as a frolic to music. Loosen up: shake, twirl, leap, stretch. You will enjoy it as much as the kids do, if you let yourself. Do your own thing, then take turns being the leader. Invent lots of arm movements.

4. IF YOUR CHILDREN are eight years old or younger, learn or make up songs and poems with motions. You probably already know some rhymes with arm movements, such as "Pattycake, Pattycake, baker's man, bake me a cake as fast as you can; roll it, pat it, mark it with a *b*, throw it in the oven for baby and me," with its final out-thrust of the arms. "Itsy-bitsy Spider" with hands climbing upward is excellent for focusing attention and lifting the energy.

5. WHAT IF you skip going to the gym once a week and instead ride bicycles with your children? Buy rain gear so you can go no matter what the weather. Notice the difference in your children's energy after a thirty-minute ride, especially if you return to a quiet house.

6. BE SURE your yard or apartment complex has sturdy swings. When you're getting dinner ready and your children are racing around the house, suggest they go out and swing for five minutes before you eat. Even better, you take a swing break with your children before you start dinner. You will *both* be calmer and more relaxed!

7. MODEL using the breath to move toward calmness. For example, say you receive a disturbing phone call. After you hang up, say to yourself so your children hear, "Okay, breathe, breathe." Sit down, shut your eyes, and take several audible long slow breaths. Your example will go much further, especially with an older child, than *telling* her to breathe when she is upset.

8. IN THE SUMMER, fill a spray bottle with filtered water and a few drops of essential oil. Lavender is calming, rosemary purifying. When your child becomes hot and whiny, offer a few sprays on the face and neck (and spray *yourself* when you feel frustrated). Keep the bottle in the refrigerator and take it with you when you run errands. It will do a lot to keep your child cheerful when getting into a hot car.

9. A WARM BATH is as calming for children as for adults. It can bring a child who has had a bad day back to his center. Do you have a hard time getting your child to want to take a bath? Offer to read aloud while he is in the bath. Or light some candles, take the CD or MP3 player into the bathroom and play relaxing music (see appendix 4), and lie down on the floor and relax while your child plays in the water. So often children just need us *with* them, available, to be satisfied and entertain themselves.

10. WHILE YOU LISTEN to a story tape or watch an appropriate video, take turns giving each other shoulder and back rubs. Use long, slow strokes up the sides of the spine and out the shoulders. Massage the base of the neck gently. Slowness is the key. Watch that your breathing is slow and regular, and your calmness will flow through your fingers.

11. STATUES is a great game to help children learn physical self-control. Play music while the family dances and frolics. Then turn the volume down and yell, "Freeze!" Everyone must freeze in the position they are in when you yell and not move a muscle until the volume goes back up. Freezing mid-movement creates some humorous results and sometimes a challenge to balance in mid-move, so it's fun. Some children will continue moving for a second or even several after the music stops; practice helps them learn control.

12. GIVE YOUR KIDS sample or travel size lotions that are scented. Encourage them to use them after their bath or whenever they want a lift. Rubbing your hands or feet with sweetly scented lotion always makes you feel better. Children will also love having their own little bottle to keep in their drawer or beside their bed.

13.   IF YOUR CHILD IS USUALLY WOUND UP when you pick him up after school or sports, try bringing a hot drink along to help settle him in cool weather. First, he must be still to hold it and drink. Then the hot milk or soy will help his energy calm down. Hot chai or even hot chocolate can help a child relax. The sugar or honey in the drink seems to be partially offset by the fat in the milk or soy, preventing it from causing a blood sugar spike.

14.   WHEN YOUR CHILD is overstimulated and cannot settle down, offer a foot rub. If your child will sit still for it, nothing is more relaxing and calming. Offer a bottle of water to drink at the same time.

You must be calmly active, and
actively calm; be intensely aware
of everything you are doing.

—Paramhansa Yogananda

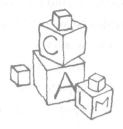

CHAPTER EIGHT
Concentrating to Calmness

ONE DAY I walked across the classroom with a paperback book balanced on my head and challenged the students, "Do any of you think you can do this?"

Of course the children were all immediately anxious to demonstrate that they could. Some students found one book easy to balance; I had them try two books on top of each other—very slippery. Others could not make it across the room without their books falling off. It was amusing to see some of the students trying to "power" their way through the feat until they finally figured out how to calm themselves to succeed. Eventually everyone was able to walk the length of the room with at least one book balanced.

Students who are successful in school know how and when to concentrate to calmness, whereas those who have difficulty in school seldom do. Danny was a good kid. He was bright and happy-go-lucky. But he had trouble with physical self-control. As much as I liked him, I could also become exasperated with his inability to be still or quiet when it was time to pay attention. Although he was not overstimulated by media, he did have inner conflicts resulting from custody battles between his parents.

Later that day, Danny was having a hard time containing himself. He kept interrupting and getting out of his seat, and he was not able to complete assignments. In a moment of frustration, I said, "Danny, I wish you'd get control of your energy."

He looked surprised. "I am in control of my energy," he replied.

"Well, okay, if you are, show me by walking with a book balanced on your head," I said.

He jumped up, eager to prove himself. Quickly he put the book on his head; he took two steps, and it fell off. He tried again, with more determination. It fell off again. Danny's face registered complete surprise; he did not know the difference between the quality of his energy then and a few hours earlier when he could balance the book. I realized that he really had no idea how different it feels inside to be calm and centered rather than out of control. Many children are out of touch with themselves in this way, lacking *intrapersonal* skills. Before Danny could learn how to calm down, he needed to be able to recognize when he was overly excited or nervous.

"How about a few slow, deep breaths?" I asked. "Or focus on one spot on the wall."

Danny did both, and after just a few breaths succeeded in balancing the book as he walked. The class applauded, and so did I. The next time I asked Danny to control his energy, he had a better idea what that meant.

calm and compassionate children

When children are bored or restless, they can become engaged and centered if you can help them to "concentrate to calmness." When overstimulated, the mind is restless, jumping from one thing to the next—but if there is sufficient motivation to focus on something, the willpower is automatically exerted to calm the body and mind. If your child takes a martial arts class, you have seen this in action, but you may not have realized *you* can engage your child's will too. You can use all sorts of little challenges to help your child concentrate to calmness and have a lot of fun doing it.

how does it work?

I know a mother of a toddler who used the "concentrate to calmness" principle proactively. To keep her child from becoming restless during a quick grocery-store stop, she gave him a nickel for each hand, telling me, "He'll concentrate on hanging on to these nickels instead of begging for everything he sees in the store." And indeed, he was so intent on holding the nickels that he showed little interest in all the displays in the market competing for his interest.

Next time your child is overstimulated, try making a game out of a concentration challenge. You might say, for example, "Can you rub your stomach clockwise and pat your head at the same time?" To do this the child must stop and focus. (It also provides a movement break, as discussed in the last chapter.) If that is easy, you can add a mental challenge too—for example, "Keep doing it and count down from ten to one." For an older child an appropriate challenge could be, "Count to twenty-one by threes." You may need to make it an active challenge: "Go find three rocks— one gray, one white, and one brown—and when you bring them to me, we'll go to the park." A verbal child will enjoy a word challenge, such as, "Can you make a new word out of the letters on that sign?"

Singing a song that requires concentration is another aid to help children settle themselves. For example, at a birthday party or in a classroom of six- or seven-year-olds, when children are scattered and unfocused, instead of raising your voice to call them all together, just get a few to sit around you and sing. Choose songs that drop words and substitute clapping, such as "B-I-N-G-O" or "Little Cabin in the Woods"; these songs require focused attention. Pretty soon all of the children will be attracted to the circle, concentrating on clapping or clicking their tongues in unison.

One of the quick games I use to engage children's attention and calm them down is Simon Says. Kids are very motivated not to be fooled (although no one is ever "out"; if a child makes a mistake, we just giggle, and everyone continues playing) and will almost always stop restless behavior to play. This kind of game is a good transition between free play time and a cooperative activity—singing "Happy Birthday" or playing a game, for example.

calm and compassionate children

engaging mental concentration

Many games and activities, including board and card games, help children develop their powers of concentration. Playing games with your children increases not only their memory, reasoning, and flexibility in thinking, but also their abilities to focus attention. That ability to focus to laser-pointed concentration is a quality they can use time and time again for every pursuit in their adult lives. Turn off the TV and get out Monopoly, the jigsaw puzzles, or the card games. I particularly recommend the game SET (available in stores and from Mindware; see appendix 4), which develops visual perception and brain processing speed.

You can play Concentration with a deck of regular playing cards. First sort the deck by the numbers of the cards. Choose two of each (two 2s, two 3s . . . two kings), shuffle, and lay the cards in a grid face down. How many you use depends on the children's age. An eleven-year-old ought to be able to work with about sixteen to twenty cards. Take turns flipping two cards over and studying their values; the point is to flip over two that are the same—you get to keep that pair. The winner is the one who has the most pairs.

A great way to develop focus with auditory memory is to say a sequence of anything to your child and have her repeat it back. It can be a number sequence; you could start with your own phone number to help your child learn it. Other great number sequences to practice are "skip counting" series, such as, "three, six, nine, twelve, fifteen;" or "four, eight, twelve, sixteen, twenty." Being able to skip count makes learning the multiplication tables easy. The series could be letters of the alphabet, random word lists, or meaningful word lists, such as, "Paris, France; London, England; Geneva, Switzerland."

Mental math not only improves a child's math skill, but is also excellent for developing concentration and the ability to focus. You ask oral math problems and the child answers quickly. For second graders you can make up simple problems such as "three plus three, minus one" or "five plus five plus two." For fourth graders, you might try, "Four times three minus two." And for sixth graders, use problems that require you to carry in your head, such as, "Eight times eight plus nine." Say the problem quickly—part of the challenge is to remember the whole problem while figuring it out. Children will often repeat the problem out loud before starting to mentally work on it; discourage this, as this usually means the child is not focusing and visualizing the problem as you say it.

Practice skills that the child is learning. For example, when he is studying fractions or percents, you could say "Ten percent of nine dollars, minus fifty cents." So that he will feel it's a game and not a test, encourage the child to make up some hard ones to ask you back! Don't do many problems at a time; if you tire him out, the child will refuse to participate. Make it fun; if there is any judgment at all when the child has difficulty, why would he want to concentrate on it?

Just a note of caution: Mentally oriented parents love these kinds of games and activities that develop one-pointed concentration, memory, and mental flexibility. But they do not develop the heart. Do not overdo it! Be sure you also offer the many kinds of activities that develop the feeling nature of your child—nature, pets, music, the arts, and just enjoying being together—and the physical body—biking, swimming, dance, and the like.

learning concentration through physical activity

Kinesthetic children will enjoy learning to concentrate more readily through the body. Sports challenges as simple as jumping rope or as complicated as executing a soccer play develop the ability to concentrate. The challenge for the teacher, parent, or coach is to pinpoint the edge of each child's skill level and challenge her to concentrate at that point, making it neither too easy nor too difficult. Martial arts classes are great for this, with their levels of achievement and emphasis on individual development. Of course, it's essential to find a teacher who understands the calm concentration part of a sport or martial arts.

A sequence of directions for children to follow is excellent because they must use the body and the brain together. Make it a game: "I bet you can't follow three directions in a row!"

When the children protest that they can too, quickly fire off a sequence for them to follow: "Back up three steps, hop on your left foot four times, and turn around." Or "Go get the book on the left end of the second shelf of the white bookcase."

Reduce or add the number of items or directions in the series so that it isn't too easy for your child's ability, but so that he can usually be successful. Then give him a turn to direct you: have your child tell you three things in a row to do. Being in charge part of the time definitely makes it fun for the child. Coming up with three directions in a logical sequence and verbalizing them requires concentration too.

You can also use songs to help kinesthetic children enjoy concentrating. All children love songs with movements, such as the "Hokey-Pokey" and the "Bunny Hop."

affirmations and meditation

Concentration can be developed through the practice of simple meditation exercises and affirmations. If you do not meditate yourself, it will probably not work for you to attempt to teach your child meditation. If you do meditate, make a few moments of meditation with your child a part of your daily routine. Teaching children to meditate is outside the scope of this book: my focus is on how to create the environment in which a child would have the inner calm to be ready to learn meditation. Having an open heart and being able to be still and silent are prerequisites for meditation, and using the first ten chapters of this book will help children with those abilities. (See appendix 4 for resources on meditation for both children and adults.)

A good time to teach a child to use affirmations is just before puberty, when the will seeks to find expression. Sandi Goodwin, the fourth and fifth grade teacher at my school, has each individual in her class come up with a goal they would like to achieve each term. It is remarkable what the children choose: sometimes it is academic, such as improving scores on spelling tests; sometimes it is something else entirely. One child determined to interrupt in class less frequently, and another to have more control over moods. Sandi works individually with the children to be sure they choose attainable goals. Then each student writes a positive affirmation, such as "I will study my spelling words for ten minutes every day," or "When I get upset, I will take a deep breath." Daily she gives them a few minutes to think about their goals and repeat their affirmations silently. It is important that they choose their own goals so that they desire success, and that she checks in often to remind them to focus on the goal. The children take pride in their progress and learn the skill of setting goals that they can use in their lives.

affirmations in daily life

The power of a child's learning affirmations was dramatically illustrated for me in a school field trip. One of the benefits of teaching in the Sierra Nevada foothills was being only an hour away from great skiing. When there were midweek specials, it was possible to take a class skiing for the day. It was an overcast day and snowing lightly as I rode up the ski lift with Chip, a twelve-year-old. It was only his second ski trip ever. We were chatting and enjoying the beautiful view of Lake Tahoe as we went uphill. As we gained altitude, we noticed the wind becoming stronger, so strong that we buttoned our coats and wrapped our scarves tighter.

Suddenly a strong gust caught the lift chair and swung us from side to side; the operator slowed the lift because of the danger. Enjoying the adventure for the most part, I glanced below to be sure we were over soft snow and not spiky trees!

Again a gust of wind blew and the lift chair lurched. Chip groaned as the ski lift ground to a halt. Noticing his white knuckles gripping the safety bar, I turned to look at him. He was paralyzed with fear, eyes wide and skin pale. "It's okay," I said, suddenly feeling a wave of fear myself as the chairs rocked and some people ahead of us screamed. I took a long breath to calm down and put my hand on his arm.

Then I heard him muttering, his eyes shut tight. I leaned closer, to hear him reciting, *"I can do everything when so I think; I can do everything when so I think."* This was a line of an affirmation I knew his class had recently learned. Was he ever applying it at the right time! I watched him muster up the will to affirm his courage rather than give in to fear. The color began to come back into his face. As we sat there on the stalled lift, he was finally able to open his eyes, chat a little, and laugh at my feeble jokes.

Seeing this boy petrified one moment, and using the tool of affirmation to take control the next, was a great experience. The best part of the story, and this is true: Chip went on to conquer his fear of heights and in high school got a job at a ski resort in order to get in as much skiing as he could!

Concentration can be physical, mental, or both. It is important to help children develop both. Young children will be most successful in concentrating if you follow up on their natural tendencies. Children who love to think will like counting challenges; children who prefer to move and master physical challenges will love to race around the house finding three items in a certain order. As children grow older, you can help them expand from their preferred mode into the other with small challenges they can easily master. Always start with easy tasks you are sure they can master, then build slowly. If you challenge some children with something they do not succeed in at first, they will often be unwilling to even try another activity. Better to work your way up, building on successes.

It is possible, however, that if children have had too little sleep, a junk food diet, or a "junk food" media mental diet, they may not have the physical and chemical resources to calm down and concentrate, no matter how motivated they may be. More about that in chapter 11.

Helping your child develop concentration gives him practice in calming himself. In addition, it is an important skill for success in school. Have fun with the practical steps!

PRACTICAL STEPS

1. TO GIVE YOUR CHILD A FOCUS, ask him to find several things and bring them back to you. For example, four different types of leaves: one dark green, one yellow-green, one gray-green, and one of a different color from those three. Or four objects whose names begin with the letters *b* or *d*.

2. IF YOU ARE in a situation in which your child cannot move—for example, sitting in an auditorium waiting for a program to begin—you can do a similar thing. The instructions are to find three things and to describe to you where they are without pointing at them. For example, find a woman in a blue shirt, three exit signs, and a person with gray hair. Or play "I Spy."

3. PURCHASE A GAME of SET and keep it in the car to pull out and play when you and one of your children have to wait somewhere, such as the dentist's office or the soccer field. SET is a game of matching patterns that develops perception, concentration, and reasoning ability. It's a game that challenges both adults and children.

4. TEACH YOUR CHILD to play Categories. Choose a category, such as food or animals for a young child. For an older child it could be a more difficult category, such as countries or boys' names. Go through the alphabet, taking turns giving an example for each letter. For example, you say "Afghanistan," the first child says "Botswana," the second, "Canada," then back to you, "Denmark," and so on.

5. ONCE A MONTH or so, have a Family Concentration Challenge Night. Start with physical challenges, such as the tree pose or balancing peas on a table knife as you walk around the house. Proceed to games such as SET, Concentration with a deck of playing cards, gin rummy, or double solitaire. End with mental games such as mental math or word play, such as Hink Pink. (Do a web search to find out what fun these are!)

6. HELP YOUR CHILD settle down by asking questions requiring a sequence of answers. For example: What are the names of your aunts and uncles from oldest to youngest? Or, tell me three different things you used a pencil for in school today, from the end of the day going backward. Or, can you name all the teachers on your hall at school, beginning from the side door and going toward the center of the building?

7. PLAY Count the Sounds. Both you and your child close your eyes and count the number of sounds you can hear. Compare notes and see who got the most; for example, the sound of the air conditioning, people talking, a faraway car engine. This game is even better for calming when you play it out in nature. Even in a city park, you can count the sounds of several different birds and maybe an insect or two, as well as the sounds of people, traffic, and more.

8. PLAY Count the Sounds in a quiet room with sounds you provide. Have your child listen, eyes shut or blindfolded, for five minutes or more and remember the sequence of the sounds. Make very quiet, peaceful sounds, such as ringing a chime softly, clicking your tongue three times, making a prolonged shhh sound, humming a few notes of a familiar song, and snapping your fingers once. Then let your child make the sounds while you listen; you both have to remember the sequence!

9. LET YOUR CHILD meditate with you for the first three or four minutes of your meditation. Watch the breath or visualize a candle.

Silence . . . gives us leave to be
great and universal.

—Ralph Waldo Emerson

CHAPTER NINE

In Silence We Know Ourselves

AT THE END OF A SCHOOL YEAR I asked Angela, a third grader, what had been her favorite field trip that year. Her class had gone on many outings, including hikes, two plays, and an adventure on a ropes course.

Angela thought for a minute and replied, "That day we hiked in the forest looking for wildflowers."

"What did you like about it?"

Looking into my eyes, she softly replied, "The quiet."

At first I was surprised at her answer. Then I reflected that Angela lived with two brothers, two dogs, a cat, and two birds. In addition, her father has a home business that brings people to the house. I could understand why she enjoyed the quiet. At a deep level, her soul probably craved it.

Inner calm needs silence and solitude to develop. In my many years as an educator, I have noticed that families whose children are calmest usually have a common characteristic: their parents have given them the gift of silence. To have time for their own thoughts, to get in touch with their own feelings, to imagine—for these pursuits children need quiet time. Media-saturated children seldom have the quality of contentment, and, unfortunately, most American kids *are* media saturated. Babies and toddlers are comfortable with silence, but as they grow older some become addicted to constant audio stimulation.

Children have little quiet or solitude in their lives unless parents make a conscious effort to provide it. Many kids get up, eat breakfast in front of the TV, and ride to school on a bus amid a crowd of children talking and shouting. Even if a child is driven to school, the parent has the radio on, or the child listens to a personal sound system. At school, children are in noisy crowds at recess, at lunch, and during class breaks. In the classroom, even if they are working quietly, there is movement—whispering, the teacher instructing another student—constant stimulation they must tune out. Then they come home and turn on the TV or the CD player! Their brains process noise and stimulation during every waking minute.

You may think that children would not like silence and would get bored quickly in the quiet. However, silence can promote creativity and inspiration; it is TV that promotes boredom and passivity. One study found that children use more calories lying on the bed daydreaming than they use watching TV. Notice how your children drag themselves off the couch after watching a couple of videos or several hours of TV.

If we want our children to become *more* aware and compassionate, we need to carefully select what they hear. A backdrop of TV and radio constantly playing leads to the exact opposite of expanding awareness. Children who are immersed in constant noise learn to block some of it out. This suppression of awareness leads to a contraction of the consciousness and sensitivity to the environment and others. On top of becoming less sensitive and aware, children's minds become filled with advertisements, song lyrics, and emotion-laden images that subconsciously affect their moods and decisions.

The underlying message from virtually all the media is that satisfying material desires and looking good will bring fulfillment. A child who watches a lot of TV also puts much time and energy into begging for the latest toy, snack item, or computer game. When she gets it, she is excited and happy, but it's an emotion that will soon fade, and she will soon move on to the next "need." This emotional high is not the kind of calm joy that comes from inner contentment. A child playing with a kitchen spoon or a few rocks may be experiencing that inner joy, tapping into his imagination; whereas a child with the most expensive, automated toy may be playing superficially—with neither his imagination or inner feeling engaged.

When families come to my school for interviews, I can often tell right away whether the child has been exposed to a lot of media. In those children, there is a restlessness, a discontent. They are constantly seeking fulfillment outside themselves. They cannot sit still; their eyes shift from object to object because they are so conditioned to flashing images that their brains have difficulty concentrating on one thing.

Contrast this child to children who live in homes with little media exposure. They play "pretend" for hours with a few blocks of wood and stuffies, creating wonderful fantasies.

They are happy with books, arts and crafts, story tapes, sports or unstructured outdoor play, and family activities. These children have patience and an ability to concentrate that few media-stimulated kids have.

remedies for restless children

I know parents who go to *extraordinary* lengths to nurture their children. They drive them to music, dance, gymnastics, and martial arts lessons and enroll them in nature, sports, and arts camps. Keeping children engaged and challenged is important, but it can be taken to an extreme. Without quiet time alone—and also quiet time with *you*—all these rich experiences can contribute to inner discontent. If you suspect this is true of your child, consider dropping some after-school activities (and the time in the car or van, usually with the radio or CD playing) and spending some of that time quietly together: playing a board game, reading and doing homework, taking a nature walk. Also be sure your child has time just to reflect, play, fantasize, daydream, and entertain himself as well.

It is true that children need time to adjust and discover the possibilities in silence. Just like the smoker who's just quit and notices at first only his cravings rather than how much better he can smell and taste, children taken off the stimulation of TV and other media stimulation will at first notice only its absence. But when children become used to amusing themselves in the quiet—with encouragement, creative playthings, and companionship—their originality and imaginations are set free in a way that is impossible if they are sitting in front of a flashing screen.

I have had students who even *requested* silence at times when they needed to concentrate. In my first years of teaching at a Living Wisdom School, I had a very lively group of nine-year-olds who chitchatted a lot when they were supposed to be working on math individually at their desks. (They were encouraged to work together; the problematic talking was about topics irrelevant to the assignment.) Because classes were small—around twelve students—we could be fairly relaxed in our classrooms, but the children were taking advantage of their freedom and getting distracted. I sought the advice of my colleague, Toby. She suggested that I challenge the children to maintain a silent period of eight to ten minutes at the beginning of their individual math work.

I asked the class how long they thought they could go without talking and got answers from one minute to thirty minutes.

"I don't think you could last even five minutes!" I countered.

"Oh, yes we can!" they vehemently replied.

"Then prove it," I challenged them.

The first few times I set a timer for five minutes, I would have to reset it several times. Someone would invariably forget and speak out in the first couple of minutes, as chatting had become a habit. After a while, though, they mastered the five-minute challenge and moved on to eight and ten minutes. I discovered that once the children had some silent time to focus, they settled in to their project or activity. There were a few children who began to remind *me* to set the timer during their math desk work.

A no talking period is very helpful in art activities, too. When doing art, children often compare their work or want to get up and see what others are doing, making them dissatisfied with their own projects and focused on each other's approval rather than enjoying their own creative process. Working the first ten minutes in absolute silence (or sometimes with soft music playing for inspiration) makes the whole class go much more smoothly. By the time the silence ends, they are content in themselves, enjoying their process. Parents can do exactly the same thing at home. Sit down to do a craft project or decorate cookies with your children and spend the first five to ten minutes working in silence. You will make discoveries you did not anticipate.

At a weeklong Education for Life seminar I taught for parents in Europe, I covered many topics—from motivating children, to nurturing feeling, to spirituality and children. At the end, I asked all the parents to come to the final session with one idea of how they would put into practice with their family something they had learned during the week. The family whose plan touched me most was an Italian couple who had a high-strung little daughter, Juliana. The dad shared that he and his wife had realized Juliana had no quiet time in her life. The parents meditated before Juliana got up in the morning. They had quiet time after she went to bed. But they now understood that their daughter had no such peace in *her* life. During all her waking hours she was either at nursery school or at home with the TV or radio on, her parents busily cooking, cleaning, and talking on the phone.

Their plan was to have silence (or relative silence) on Saturday mornings. They planned to eliminate music, radio, and TV; they would turn the phone *off*, and they would not use the time to discuss their plans or issues. Their interactions with Juliana would include quiet play, concentration games, and talking about what was happening in her life and how she felt about it. They would give her creative materials, and they would draw, cut, glue, and create alongside her.

What a wonderful change in this little girl's life! Unfortunately, her parents, small-business owners, could not do this every night. But I believe that even withdrawing from their busyness once a week *with* Juliana would help her grow more relaxed and calm.

different personalities benefit from silence

My friend and colleague Lorna Knox has three children. I asked her about their need for silence. She told me that her oldest, who is a very thoughtful person, really needs some solitude without the stimulation of TV and other kids. He retreats to his room to read, or play story tapes, or build with his LEGO set until he feels ready to face the world again. When he needs quiet solitude he gets moody, but as he has gotten older he knows this about himself, and he will even turn down time with his friends if he has had "too much."

Although children differ in their need for downtime to be inside themselves, depending on whether they are more introspective or sociable by nature, all children need that time. Lorna went on to describe her second child:

"Timothy, the seven-year-old, is much more sociable and believes he needs input from others to have fun. But I have learned to structure quiet time for him, although a bit more subtly. He thinks sitting in the dark is special, and he will listen to music in the dark or just lie on his bed and think.

"I was worried about Mary, my youngest, getting quiet time because she is the third child and just isn't alone much. But she really blossoms when the boys are not home. She will play alone for long periods and seems to relax because she is not worried about being interrupted or pleasing anyone but herself. When my husband and the boys are out in the evening, she takes long baths and does things at her own pace."

Lorna's three children have widely differing temperaments, but all benefit from quiet time and introspection. A very social personality may need less alone time than an introspective child, but even the social child needs to learn to find contentment in being alone. A child who does not learn that skill may grow up to be a person who seeks any company, even that of inappropriate companions, rather than enjoying her own time for thought and relaxation.

silence is essential to self-knowledge

The skill of introspection helps us develop the self-control that leads to kindness. As part of their mystical tradition, most religions teach us the necessity of being alone in silence. In Judaism, this tradition is called *hitbodedut*, a form of prayer in solitude that leads to self-transcendence. In yoga it is called *pratyahara*, the interiorization of the mind. In *The Way of Reflection*, Saint Teresa of Avila calls it the Prayer of Quiet. She says the soul is conscious of this state "which is a deep and peaceful happiness . . . [and which] . . . differs from the happiness of the world."

It is only in quiet that we can develop the side of ourselves that Howard Gardner, author of several books on multiple intelligences, calls *intrapersonal intelligence*. According to Gardner, "Intrapersonal intelligence refers to having an understanding of yourself, of knowing who you are, what you can do, what you want to do, how you react to things, which things to avoid, and which things to gravitate toward. We are drawn to people who have a good understanding of themselves because those people tend not to screw up. They tend to know what they can do. They tend to know what they can't do. And they tend to know where to go if they need help."

It takes energy and effort to provide your child or class with the quiet and peace in which inner calmness and self-awareness can develop. There is such an emphasis on intellectual stimulation and entertainment for children that solitude and downtime are neglected or even scorned. Of course, children benefit from rich, varied experiences and exposure to many different kinds of activities, but consider balancing the "busyness" of our contemporary lifestyle with periods of silence.

1. EASE THE TRANSITION away from too much media (TV, computer games, radio) by substituting calming music (see appendix 4 for suggestions) until your family's restlessness calms down enough to tolerate silence.

2. PUT THE TV in the attic. Okay, you don't have to be that radical. Just limit TV to one hour a day. Chances are you will find this quite challenging, because TV seems to be habit-forming. Then, after limiting it for a while, try a TV-free month. Unplug the TV and put it away so it requires a lot of effort to get it out; just unplugging it will probably not work. If you can successfully do this, I promise that your view about TV's effect on your family will change. You will then be in a position to make a really informed decision about how much TV to allow.

3. LOOK AT YOUR FAMILY'S DIET. Sugar and caffeinated drinks make it *difficult* for most children and *impossible* for some to be physically or mentally quiet.

4. BE SURE your child is getting enough exercise and outside play time. It is asking too much of a child to be calm and quiet if there is pent-up physical energy needing expression.

5. DEMONSTRATE that you value silence and solitude your-self. If your life is so frenetic that you never stop to take stock and introspect, how can your children learn to be quiet? If you always read, meditate, journal, or pray *after* your child goes to bed, he does not see one of the most important activities you can share.

6. SPEND TIME in nature together as a way to wind down from your daily demands.

7. DEVELOP QUIET ACTIVITIES you can share with your children. When you provide the space and companionship, children can spend hours building with a LEGO set, creating fairylands with a few sticks and pieces of moss, painting murals on butcher paper tacked to the garage wall. Their imagination is the only limit!

8. CUT BACK on optional activities. Some children thrive on challenge and have so much energy that many after-school activities, plus weekend activities, feed them. But for the majority of children, being scheduled more days than not is overstimulating. Use the years from kindergarten through third grade to try out one activity at a time—such as music, dance, art, gymnastics, and soccer or other sports—and let your child's interests emerge.

9. MAKE A COMMITMENT to sit down with your children at least twice a week and share a real-world, not a virtual-world, activity with them. To replace TV, movies, and computer games, you can work jigsaw puzzles, perform music, read aloud, or play games that are fun and challenging, such as Cranium, SET, or that old standby, Monopoly. (See appendix 4 for resources.) This is essential if you are beginning to create a quiet household without media, because children will need your attention while they adjust.

10.   TRY SILENCE CHALLENGES. Make a game out of it. Set a timer and see if you and your children can go without saying a word for five minutes—or if that is easy, for ten! Try this in particular at the beginning of a craft project or board game or jigsaw puzzle. You will be pleased at how everyone's concentration and enjoyment will increase.

"Life will always be full of ups and downs," my grandmother used to say. "But you don't have to go up and down with them. You can teach your mind to be calm and kind whatever comes."

—Eknath Easwaran,
Original Goodness

CHAPTER TEN

Claiming Personal Power

BEING CALM AND COMPASSIONATE does not mean being namby-pamby. Helen Gorman, our kindergarten teacher, recently saw the Dalai Lama in Dharamsala. He strode briskly onto the stage with great energy, reminding her of the late saint, Paramhansa Yogananda, who used to run onto the stage, and demand, "How is everybody?" The audience would enthusiastically reply, "Awake and ready!" We can guess that the Christ who stood up to the Pharisees at the temple must have been charismatic and strong—as well as gentle and compassionate.

In 1990 I met Mother Teresa at her ashram in Delhi. Confounding my expectations of a soft-spoken tender personality, she too strode into the room with determination. As she spoke, I could feel her dynamic willpower. Although she was physically tiny, she had such powerful magnetism that it was easy to see how she founded a worldwide work. Meeting her helped me understand that unconditional love goes hand in hand with great energy and self-control. For compassionate behavior to appear attractive to boys, in particular, they must understand that courage and inner strength go hand in hand with it.

power to show empathy

A couple of summers ago I was camping on the Oregon coast. From my campsite I could barely see two brothers playing in the trees, just beyond piles of brush and a thicket of briars. The campsites surrounded this overgrown area. Before long, I heard the younger child yelling, "Help me, help me, I can't get out!" Peering through the brush, I realized he must have fallen into a hole or depression. "Mom, Dad, help me!"

His older brother, about ten years old, stood frozen, looking down helplessly at the younger child. As I looked in vain for a way to get to them, I heard the parents calling, "We're coming, we're coming." Still, the older brother made no an effort to help the smaller child, not even kneeling down by the hole to comfort or calm him. The parents finally arrived and pulled the younger child out. Unhurt, he calmed down quickly as the parents carried him away. The big brother followed, head bowed, hands stuffed in his pockets.

I felt sorry for him, as he so obviously felt ineffectual in this situation. Even if he could not have helped the younger child out of the hole, his inability to reassure his brother was a sharp contrast to the children I am used to. Parents of kindergartners and first graders in our school comment on the kindness and gentleness of our older children. The mother of a first grader told me that on her son's first day of soccer practice, she was surprised that the older boys ignored the younger, unlike the boys at our school, who usually greet the younger ones, "What's up? How ya doin'?" and encourage them in games.

This supportive culture is developed consciously: by encouraging the older children's abilities and desire to be useful, by sharing with them our delight at the cute things the younger ones do and say, and by giving them avenues to get to know the younger children so they feel comfortable with them. In the fall, two older children at a time go over to the preschool to "play" with the little ones. The preschool teacher plans activities that the older children can join in on. At an all-school assembly in October, one of the older students introduces each preschooler and each new kindergartner to the rest of the school. If the little ones are too shy to come up front, the older ones stand by each child at his seat and tell us about the child—family, pets, and favorite foods. The connections are continued during the year when the preschool teacher brings her class over to visit the upper class's pet lizard.

A family could do a version of our secret pal project to help children expand their sympathies to younger ones. Every February, students in the oldest class "adopt" children from kindergarten as a secret pal. They write them notes and bake them treats, and when the little ones are outside at recess, they sneak into their room and leave the surprises. The kindergartners come up with all kinds of fantastic speculations about who their secret pals might be. The older children really enjoy this activity, even though they don't get thanked directly because it remains a secret who the pals are. Their joy is in making the little ones happy.

These kinds of opportunities create a culture in which the older children enjoy being mature enough to include the little ones on the playground occasionally. They are tolerant of the funny things the young children say and do and never mock them, and they don't hesitate to help out if a younger child falls or needs assistance. They know they are capable and compassionate, and they show it in many situations.

One day I observed Stephen, a kindergartner, coming out of the bathroom and pausing in the hallway to watch two older boys practicing guitar. One of the boys noticed him. "You want to sing with us, Steve?" They continued to practice as Stephen made up some sort of off-key song with nonsense words to go along with their accompaniment. He then skipped off to his room, pleased with himself, while the older boys smiled at each other, silently sharing amusement and affection for the little boy.

I would caution you not to attempt to make siblings have this kind of relationship unless they are at least five or six years apart. Parents have to use discretion because it can create resentment to ask the older child to put aside his own desires prematurely when they conflict with those of a younger sibling. It is important to pick moments when children feel open to ask them to extend themselves, and you should never make them feel guilty when they do not feel sympathy. Otherwise, you would be encouraging the older child to develop resentment rather than empathy.

showing children their personal power

Our emotions, moods, and restlessness can prevent us from being calm and compassionate. Sometimes it takes an act of will to overcome those obstacles and behave with awareness of the needs of others. Good parents and teachers do this every day. Great parents and teachers teach their children that they, too, have the power to control themselves.

I was visiting our primary class one day. One little girl—an eager learner, full of mental and physical energy—talked incessantly. She had difficulty giving other children a chance to participate. The teacher asked her several times not to interrupt. The third time she barged into a conversation, Karen said, "Cecilia, you know I said you'd have to work by yourself if you interrupted again."

Cecilia replied, "I know, but Karen, I just can't stop talking!" She looked pleadingly at her teacher, hoping for a reprieve.

Then Karen made a brilliant observation, "Yes you *can* help it, Cecilia, because *you are a strong, powerful little girl.* And you can use that power to control your talking. Now I want you to take your work to the quiet area and think about that."

As Karen called her strong and powerful, Cecilia's eyes got big as if she had just heard a new and foreign concept. She smiled as she thought of herself as powerful. In a few minutes she rejoined the class, quietly. Over time, with firm, consistent guidance, Cecilia did put forth the effort to raise her hand and take turns—not for approval or from fear of punishment, but because those around her helped her realize she had the ability to control herself.

It is so easy to disempower children when we are teaching them right from wrong; for example, when we force them to apologize for something when they are still feeling resentful and not at all apologetic. This takes away from them the opportunity to practice apologizing sincerely out of a feeling of regret.

Sometimes parents, out of love and enjoying the feeling of being needed, do too much for their children, and the kids end up feeling inadequate to act for themselves. We should always be looking for ways to give our children tasks they can succeed at and that contribute to the family or the classroom. This can be accomplished in the smallest of ways. For example, when the child is a toddler, you can ask that he hand you an item out of your reach and then thank him for being helpful. You can give him an item to carry from your grocery bag. It is wonderful to have a spirit of service toward your children, but it is taking it too far if we do not help them learn to use their abundant energy to help themselves and others.

A Living Wisdom School administrator, Michael Nitai Deranja, tells about how he helped his daughter develop her willpower and belief in herself, by seldom giving her unneeded things outright but by making them available if she put out effort. His policy was that if she asked for something he felt was not essential, but not unreasonable either (such as a ten-speed instead of a thrift-store bike, or expensive athletic shoes instead of the ordinary brand), he would pay for half, but she would have to pay for the other half.

Then he would give her opportunities to work, earn the money, and experience the satisfaction of achieving goals.

When we are teaching children values to live by, it is important that we show them they have the inner power not only to do the right thing, but also to know what the right thing is. Sandi Goodwin helps children to develop their discrimination in many ways. I overheard a conversation between her and a student who approached her during lunch. He told her what some other child was doing on the playground. Sandi stopped him. "Do you remember the difference between tattling and telling?"

Jason paused as he tried to remember. "Oh, yeah. Telling the truth is when you are trying to be helpful and protect someone from getting hurt, and tattling is when you are trying to get someone in trouble."

"Which are you doing now, Jason?"

Again he paused as he looked for his own motives. Suddenly, he grinned. "Never mind," he said, running off to play. (Please note that by "getting hurt" we mean not only physical hurts, but hurt feelings as well.) Of course, the desired outcome is for children to be intrinsically motivated to be compassionate to others. However, most of us need to learn that we can choose to do what we think is right even when we do not feel compassion.

healing prayers

An even more subtle type of personal power is the power to help others through prayer and positive energy. You can tell your child about the scientific studies that show that heart patients who are prayed for improve faster than those who are not, even if none of the patients know whether or not they are being prayed for. Every family knows someone who is troubled by ill health or other challenges. You can suggest praying for them together.

If you don't have your own ritual for healing prayers, you can use the technique we use at our school. We close our eyes and call to mind each person to whom we wish to send healing energy (kids love to pray for their pets too!). We might say something like, "Picture Grandma in your mind. Surround her with healing light. Visualize beautiful golden light all around her and see her smiling peacefully. Let's rub our hands together and hold them up, visualizing light streaming out from our fingertips and going to Grandma and filling her with peace." Then we chant "Peace," "Shanti," or "Aum" as we imagine that healing energy.

Children discover a place of sweet compassion in their hearts by the practice of healing prayers; plus, they realize they are not helpless even if there is nothing they can do outwardly. It may take several times for your child to get into the flow of it, but in my experience nearly *every* child enjoys being a channel for sending love to others in this way. If you teach your child to pray for others, be sure to explain that the outcome may not be what we wish. There may be no obvious change or healing, but the person we pray for may feel more peaceful or more open to love.

On a field trip, riding the light rail to downtown Portland, several children and I sat side by side facing the middle of the car. I noticed one of the girls watching a couple sitting to our right just beyond the doors. The couple's clothes, their hair, their possessions were dirty. They were also acting strangely, growling and muttering, and when they looked up, their eyes looked crazed. Certain that they were on drugs, I felt the only danger they posed was to themselves. Gradually the children became aware of their bizarre behavior, and they fell silent as they tried not to stare.

Wondering how I could help the kids relax, I remembered Lorna Knox's axiom of how to react to scary events—open your heart to even more love. I leaned over and whispered to the kids, "I think they're on drugs and have taken too much; we can't do anything about it, but it might help them if we silently send them peace and light." The children were relieved at being able to take some action, and their apprehension vanished as they quietly visualized light around the unfortunate couple.

Our prayers for others help those prayed for and also replace our fear with the courage that comes from empathy. Opportunities abound in our modern lives to show our children how to choose light and love rather than fear and tension. For example, when you are out driving and you pass an accident with paramedics on the scene, you and your child can visualize light and healing energy around any injured people, wishing them well.

Developing the habit of consciously sending others goodwill and positive intentions at a young age gives children a skill they can use throughout their lives—a skill that not only helps others, but that also *calms themselves.*

replacing fear or insecurity with compassionate action

Helping others by concrete means is important too, of course. At our school, the older children select charities to which they give 5 to 10 percent of all they earn from their field-trip fundraising. Past recipients have included Ronald McDonald House and Mother Miracle School in India. It is good for children to learn they can influence the world positively, whether by collecting food for a food bank or by giving car washes to raise funds.

Currently in American culture, it is popular for children to raise money for victims of disaster or, for example, to send gifts such as school supplies to hurricane victims. Discussing wars, disasters, disease, and social problems with preteens and teens and finding ways they can contribute is not only appropriate but also essential to their development as calm and compassionate people.

However, as pointed out in chapter 5, it is better to *limit exposure to tragic events* for younger children—up to age eleven or so. Protecting children from bad news is not always possible, however. If your child finds out about violence in the news and is asking questions or talking about it, you can be sure they need reassurance. It gives a child confidence in his ability to cope to do something that helps the victims; for instance, collecting bottles and cans to recycle and sending the funds to a relief agency. You can help children learn to respond with their inner power of empathy and compassion, teaching them to expand their sympathy to others, rather than to dwell on their own fear. For example, if a person known to your children is killed or injured in war, this would be a great time to have children write letters of support to other personnel in the armed services. However, you should not feel it's necessary to tell them about a violent death if they are unaware of it.

Guiding children to compassionate action toward those in need who are in their immediate circle is important. Your child will learn more about love and empathy by regularly stopping by to see a lonely elderly neighbor with you than by donating to far-off disaster relief. Being friendly to a child who is often teased or left out by the in-group requires far more compassion than helping people we do not know. Coming up with creative ways to give assistance to those in your everyday life is challenging; encouraging your child in this direction—or better yet, showing by example—helps our children learn how to expand their sympathies.

I appreciated the reaction of my friend Lorna's family to the devastating news of the sudden death of their teenage neighbor. Lorna found a rose variety with the same name as the deceased girl. The whole family drove all the way to Canada to purchase that rose. They brought it back and planted it in the neighborhood as a show of sympathy to the family. Although Lorna's children suffered the loss of a friend, they also learned that they have the power to act with love in the face of tragedy.

confidence through affirmations

The power of positive thinking and visualizing desired outcomes has been documented in the fields of health and sports. Michael Jordan has said that as he made a shot in the last second of a tied game he *never* thought, "What would happen if I miss?" He only saw himself making the shot. If you have not practiced affirmations yourself, get a good book on them (see appendix 4) and begin!

Children can begin to learn to speak positively about themselves at a young age. Put-downs should be treated as seriously when they are aimed at oneself as when they are aimed at someone else.

For example, at our school, if children say, "I'm so stupid!" they are gently corrected. We may reply, "You may feel frustrated, but you are not stupid. Please tell me you're feeling frustrated."

When a child in kindergarten or first grade says, "I can't do it," we may answer gently, "Say, 'I haven't learned to do it *yet.*'" By the time they are in third or fourth grade, they seldom waste energy asserting that they *cannot* do anything, because they know that positive thinking helps them learn.

As children get older (fourth grade on up) we teach them how to use affirmations to accomplish their goals. Telling stories of athletes who use visualization helps to convince them that this is an activity worth doing. It is important that children *choose* what they want to improve so their will is engaged, not coerced. If a child has learned to use affirmations, she will remember them later when she needs them, just as Chip did on the ski lift (chapter 8).

A teacher at the Nevada City Living Wisdom School had her fifth and sixth graders each choose a quality they wanted to develop and write their own affirmations. Later they put a few of them to music and recorded them. I wish every preteen could internalize this one written by an eleven-year-old boy:

Courage to take the first new step;
New faces and new places I can accept.
Brave and exciting. Have the courage to be strong.
I KNOW I CAN

PRACTICAL STEPS

1. DO YOUR CHILDREN have younger cousins, or do you have neighbors with younger children? Encourage your children to see the sweetness and vulnerability of these children and plan projects that offer opportunities to delight them. Your children can leave a bag of treats on the neighbor's front porch the night before Valentine's Day with a note from "your secret pal." Throw a tea party for the little ones or invite them to share pizza, or have your children invite them over to see something special, such as a bird's nest or a new kitten.

2. ENCOURAGE YOUR CHILD to realize her own power to be helpful by asking her to do little things for others, even if you could do them yourself. For example, if you are approaching a door at the same time as an elderly person, instead of holding it open yourself, ask your child, "Can you open the door and hold it for that man carrying a package?" If your child is too small to do that herself, do it together, verbalizing your actions: "Come help me hold the door for this gentleman."

3. TEACH YOUR CHILD to relax and take control of his own reactions when you hear an ambulance or fire truck on the road. As you pull over to give the emergency vehicle clearance, you can say, "Let's pray for the firefighters that they will be safe." Send them courage, and visualize light around the people in an ambulance or fire truck as it passes by. You will find this a great way to transform the body's instinctive stressful reaction to the sound of loud sirens.

4. WHEN your son or daughter complains that another child has treated him unfairly or does not want to play, focus on your child's power to choose to be happy anyway. Never ignore evidence that your child is being bullied, but realize that if you intervene in every little childhood rejection, you are teaching your child that being liked is more important than being in charge of one's own moods.

5. HELP your children develop the capacity to channel their willpower by putting goals just a bit out of reach and then challenging them to achieve them by offering to match their efforts.

6. MAKE IT a family activity to try out the effectiveness of affirmations. Each family member chooses something to work on and writes an affirmation. Possibilities include "I am learning to jump rope and getting better every time I practice" or "I breathe deeply when a colleague at work challenges me, and I know no one can disturb my inner calm." Each evening at dinner, share times during the day that you were able to practice your affirmation when you needed it. You could also do a whole family affirmation such as, "We are calm and compassionate!"

7. TRY THIS experiment together to show your children how the energy they give out determines what comes back. As you shop and pass people in the aisles, count the number of people who smile at you. The next time you go to the store, smile at everyone first, and count the number of people who smile at you.

8. WHEN YOUR CHILD makes a mistake in judgment and treats someone poorly, as you talk to him about it, reassure him that you know he has to make mistakes to learn. Assure him that he has the power to choose love and compassion, even when it is hard to do. Always assume that he can improve and that any mistakes are made out of self-absorption, not meanness.

Part Three

Surrounding Influences

THE PREVIOUS TEN CHAPTERS have described different arenas in which you can engage children in opening their hearts, feeling peace, and learning to focus. The final two chapters are not about your children, but about all that surrounds them and contributes to or detracts from their calmness and compassion.

Chapter 11 addresses factors that parents can control to some degree and that exert great influence on children, including

- Nutrition (physical diet)
- Media (mental diet)
- Peer influences
- School culture
- The acquisition mentality

And finally, keep in mind that *you* are the most important influence of all on your children's capacity for love and serenity. Chapter 12 discusses the importance of your own peace of mind and makes suggestions on how you can become calmer and more compassionate with your children. A wit said, "It's noble to change yourself. But it is nobler to change others . . . and a whole lot easier!"

It is tempting to think that when our children are agitated and selfish, we need only to change them. But we will have more success if we first examine our own ability to relax and be dispassionate. The more serenity we have, the more calm our children can be.

Our children need a nest of caring to shelter from the outside. And likewise, they need an infusion of higher energy to nurture the intuition and creativity that are each child's birthright.

—Mary Belknap,
Homo deva: Evolution's Next Step

CHAPTER ELEVEN

Environment Matters

OUR SUMMER CAMPERS were hiking up Rooster Rock, a steep hill composed of volcanic material in the Columbia Gorge. The views were spectacular. A low stone retaining wall edged some of the switchbacks bordering steep drops. Crafted in the WPA era, the two-foot-high wall contained little arches like portholes or windows in some places. As we approached one of them, a nine-year-old girl knelt down and looked toward the vista of the Columbia River through the little arch. Then she said, "This is a baby-suicide hole."

Startled, I said, "What do you mean?"

"Well, a baby could jump through here and commit suicide."

I mulled this over for the next several hundred feet of the climb. Why would these dark thoughts be in the mind of a nine-year-old girl whose parents I knew to be kind, loving people? Where had this child gotten such morbid images that overshadowed her awareness of our beautiful surroundings? A possibility occurred to me.

"Do you like movies?" I asked her.

"Oh, yes."

"Do you get to watch videos?"

"All the time. I watch with my big brother."

"How old is he?

"Oh, sixteen. We watch everything."

Adolescent boys do not usually choose romance comedies or family movies. The columnist Leonard Pitts Jr. said, "What's frightening is that, as a father pulls them [his teen sons] toward higher ground, they are pulled in another direction by a pop culture . . . that is materialist, misogynistic, pornographic and violent." Although he was speaking specifically of hip-hop, his characterization describes much of the entertainment culture.

It was clear to me that this girl had a mental diet of R-rated images, violence, and gore. Her family and her brothers were unaware of how the images and emotions of such movies were affecting her nine-year-old consciousness.

hothouse flowers?

You may be reluctant to stand up against the mainstream even if you dislike the influences of consumerism and mass media on your children. Children beg to buy or see what "everybody else gets to" and some parents back down from their initial refusal because they equate material abundance with happiness. Other parents may be reluctant to enforce limitations because they fear friends and family will think them weird or conservative and uptight. Others are afraid

calm and compassionate children

of raising children who, like hothouse flowers, are too fragile to thrive in the real world.

Children are especially open and receptive to the feeling messages from the arts. They keenly feel both dark, defiling depictions of violence and meaninglessness and the inspiration of uplifting stories, films, and theater. By exposing children to uplifting, beautiful artistic expressions, we allow their hearts and minds to be filled with positive thoughts. If we expose them to art that is violent or depressing, they will either take on these moods themselves because they are so open, or they will start to shut down the heart in order to protect themselves. I have heard a few parents say that children need to develop a "tough skin" or "learn to take it" because the world is like that. However, when the heart closes, it closes to the positive influences as well as the negative.

The idea that we need to put children in environments that will toughen them up so they can cope with later life is false. You would not make a three-year-old sit at a desk for an hour a day because he will have to do it in first grade. You wait until he is developmentally ready. Before permitting our children to witness violence, cruelty, and sexual activity, we need to help them develop self-understanding and the skills for living that will help them recognize what choices lead them to happiness.

Children who are prematurely exposed to fear, violence, and hatred have problems later on, because their natural development into loving adults has been thwarted. It is true that we do not want to deprive children of the opportunity of learning the skills to overcome obstacles by controlling *every* part of their lives. We want children to have challenges to master; those may be academic for some children and athletic, musical, or social for others. But it is also true that, even if we provide an entirely loving, safe, secure environment, people and situations *will* arise that challenge them. Adults who remember childhood as an idyllic time of life are remembering the inner joy and forgetting their childhood disappointments, anxieties, and fears that almost everyone experiences.

To prepare children for later life experiences, we need to teach them how to meet challenges with a positive attitude, rather than either fighting their battles for them or dismissing their feelings by not taking their obstacles seriously. Parents should provide the safety zone in which their children can figure out how to handle these difficulties. Do everything you can to ensure your child's environment promotes the values you espouse, especially up to the age of puberty when they will be ready to explore, try out different roles, and test their decision-making skills.

media

Countless research studies have been done that illustrate the power of media for both good and ill. One often-quoted study by Dr. David McClelland found that when students watched documentaries about Mother Teresa, their immune system was strengthened; there were significant increases in salivary immunoglobulin. Conversely, when children

calm and compassionate children

watch violence, their muscles tense and their bodies secrete adrenaline and cortisol, substances that put the body on alert for danger. Calm children are relaxed, not tense. In the days when there were only four TV networks, the faculty of the public school where I worked noticed that the day after an especially violent film aired, the atmosphere of the entire school would be affected. Children were agitated, loud, and unable to concentrate well.

A study reported in the April 2004 issue of *Pediatrics* showed that for every hour of daily TV watched at ages one through three, the incidence of attention problems at age seven increased *10 percent!* Attention problems included difficulty concentrating, restlessness, and impulsivity. As I mentioned in chapter 9, when prospective families bring their five-year-olds to visit our school, I can usually tell within the first five minutes of the interview whether or not the child has a steady diet of TV, movies, and video games. Children who are media-saturated are restless, with quick eye movements, seeking stimulation, whereas children who do not watch TV are much more calm and attentive, with steady eyes.

While at the High Desert Museum in Bend, Oregon, I sat on a bench and watched children from several schools pass through the display of a re-created gold mine and mining shack. A working telescope was outside the shack. The children who noticed it usually spent at least a couple of minutes focusing it and looking through it at other visitors. One boy ran through the exhibit, not stopping to observe anything. Reaching the door of the shack, he spotted the telescope and grabbed it. He crouched down, but instead of looking through it, he began making machine-gun noises as he splayed it back and forth, "aiming" toward classmates and teachers. The potential of using the instrument as a telescope was lost on him; he never tried looking through it. I wondered how many TV shows he had watched and how many violent video games he had played. His perception of reality, like the little girl's on the hiking trail, was skewed by images imprinted in his brain.

Children up to the age of about eleven or twelve who have not been jaded by exposure to violence live much more in the heart than adults do. They love inspirational stories; they naturally respond to nature, especially to animals; and they feel their kinship with all life. They resonate with the Native Americans who called the other earth creatures "animal people" and "plant people." During the early years, before puberty, is the time for the adults around them to nurture that awareness and not allow them to watch adult movies and TV. We do not show all of reality to a child who isn't emotionally ready any more than we would give a knife to a three-year-old who doesn't yet have the physical skills and ability to use it safely.

The American Pediatrics Association recommends *no* television for children under age two and strict limits as children get older. I go further to recommend no TV or movies at all for children under three and very little after that until the child is school age, when a video or a children's program or movie once a week would be appropriate. By the time the child reaches nine years old, twice a week is fine, as long as the content of the programs is monitored. Unsupervised Internet access and violent video

calm and compassionate children

games are even more potentially dangerous to your child's development.

Many families have found that attempting to limit TV viewing becomes a source of argument and negotiation. A much simpler and easier (long-term) solution is to just have no TV at all. Removing temptations entirely, some families I know don't get cable and don't own an antenna! Other families with students in our school simply put the TV in a closet where it is rolled out only on rare occasions to watch a DVD or special programming. Perhaps you can make no TV more palatable by putting the money you save on cable fees in savings to purchase something the family will enjoy together—for example, camping gear, a play structure for the yard, or a pet.

Does it sound impossible to turn off the TV permanently? Then think seriously about dependency. Who in your family is addicted to TV? What sort of energy and time would be freed up without it? Can you lock it up for two weeks as an experiment and notice the results?

One parent who created a TV-free household told me that she could not have foreseen how much her children would calm down and how much fun they would have once their craving to be passively entertained subsided. If children already have the habit, at first they will certainly rebel against no TV. It is a bit more conceivable to them if you talk not in terms of what you are taking away, but in terms of what you are gaining:

- Time in the evening for games
- Playing music together
- Helping with homework

- Doing art or craft projects
- Reading aloud together
- Playing concentration games (see chapter 9)
- Playful wrestling
- Giving each other foot or back rubs

Then live up to your promises; spend that time together as a family, or one-on-one with individual children, taking turns. "Love means spending time with kids. . . .We need emotionally intimate time and *shared activity* [my emphasis] to keep any relationship—between spouses, between parents and kids—strong and growing," says Tom Lickona, author and parent, in *Character Matters*. Not only will your children's creativity and curiosity blossom, but you will be rewarded with closer relationships and a more harmonious household.

peers

If your children are already eight or older, you have found out how influenced they are by the choices of their friends and peers. They are attracted to the toys, food, and entertainment that the most magnetic and popular members of their peer group endorse. Finding like-minded families with whom you can socialize helps forestall this attraction. Building a community of children and parents with similar lifestyles will keep your child from feeling deprived or isolated by your choices.

It is interesting to watch the way that different personalities and temperaments of children interact. In the classroom, teachers find out which children make good partners and which should never sit together because they bring out the worst in each other. Sasha, a ten-year-old in my school, regularly plays with two different girls. Sasha's mother said that when one friend comes over, she hears laughter and even singing coming from her daughter's room. The girls' imaginative play lasts for hours without a break. When the other child comes over, she hears no laughter, and within an hour the children are coming to her, whining, "We're bored. Let's go somewhere or get a video." Of course, she schedules more play dates with the girl with whom her child expresses creativity and joy.

Parents should be alert to the effects different playmates have on their child. What may seem merely annoying— your son comes in with bad language or teases a younger sibling after playing with a particular friend—may be a warning sign. When your child is with these playmates away from you, their negative behavior can quickly escalate into antisocial and dangerous behaviors, such as bullying or throwing objects at cars. No matter how sweet, kind, and well-behaved your child is, if he socializes with children who do not hold your values, he can be lured into trouble. As long as you still have an influence, choose companions and activities that keep his energy at least positive—and at best, calm and compassionate.

According to the Index of Leading Cultural Indicators, in the thirty-year period between 1960 and 1990, while our standard of living was rising, the teen suicide rate *tripled*.

The American standard of living is the highest in the world, but it does not follow that we are happy. Disenchantment with the empty promise of happiness that corporate American advertising portrays has spawned a yearning for deeper meaning and a movement toward simplicity. Popular book titles reflect this; for example, *Living Simply with Children* by Marie Sherlock and *The Progress Paradox: How Life Gets Better While People Feel Worse* by Gregg Easterbrook.

An overabundance of material possessions will not make a child happy; in fact, it contributes to unhappiness. Some children are so inundated with stuff that they have no space for their creativity or imagination to flower. A parent who buys everything a child wants soon finds that the child is whining daily for the next new thing, another "fix." When she gets what she wants, the child is temporarily excited that her desire is fulfilled, but that excitement never lasts long. By buying too much, the parent communicates that satisfaction can be gained through things. In *Inner Simplicity*, Elaine St. James explains, "this excess of gift giving . . . complicates the children's lives . . . numbs their sensitivity, and their creativity. . . . It also sets up unrealistic expectations that can never be fulfilled in the real world."

I was delighted when my niece told me how she and her husband handled Christmas Day. Like most young parents, they had bought Christmas presents for their eighteen-month-old son. More gifts from friends, grandparents, and aunts and uncles waited under the tree. The big gift Benjamin was getting was a retro fire truck big enough to sit in and pedal around the house. When he came downstairs on Christmas morning and saw his bright red truck, his eyes got big. After a brief pause, he climbed in and was off. He laughed and chattered and did not want to get out of it, even for breakfast.

He was having such a good time that my niece and her husband decided any more gifts would be unnecessary and probably overwhelming, so they did not give him any more until the next day. For them it was a lovely Christmas, free of overexcitement and exhaustion. Benjamin could not have been any happier, and by the time I got there to see him in mid-January, his eagerness to play with his fire truck had not yet worn out.

nutrition

Why is nutrition in a chapter on environment? Part of the environment your child must live in is the body through which she feels, moves, thinks, and acts. In chapter 7 I mentioned the importance of exercise, to keep both body and mind from being restless. Diet is equally important. Poor foods, high in processed carbohydrates, prevent focus and concentration because they cause the blood sugar to peak and fall. Moodiness, whining, low energy, hyperkinetic energy, and mental fogginess can be the result of food choices.

One of Sandi's students sat slouched in his desk, moodily complaining about his assignment. Knowing he was usually a bright and energetic student, Sandi tried to jolly him out of his mood, but it didn't work. Finally I heard her ask, "What did you have for breakfast?"

"We were running late, so we stopped for donuts."

A few other kids exclaimed, "Lucky!"

"And hot chocolate," he added.

That boy was delighted to have donuts and hot chocolate. But he wasn't lucky. If his dad had observed his son's inability to participate that morning, maybe he would bring a jar of nut butter in the car next time!

Our teachers know from the experience of many overnight field trips that when we are lax about controlling the children's diets, letting them indulge in sugar and lots of processed food, they become either moody or hyper. When we provide only proteins, grains, and fruits and veggies, the trip always goes much more smoothly. Foods that fuel blood sugar spikes and lows hinder children from being either calm or compassionate. It is difficult to have empathy for others when your body chemistry is unstable.

You have to be vigilant to give your child healthy food. Public awareness of healthy eating is increasing, but the biggest change so far has been in marketing, not actual improvement of the products. For example, the name of the cereal Sugar Pops has been changed to just Pops. Sugar Smacks are now just Smacks, and Sugar Frosted Flakes have dropped the word *sugar* too. But look at the contents: sugars are still the number-one ingredient.

After your child begins school, his diet will be influenced by his peers. However, if you have provided only healthy food up until then, he will probably continue to enjoy those foods when away from his peers. Gradually, he will learn to recognize how his body feels after eating different foods if you point it out gently, without judgment.

schooling

Unless you homeschool your children, school peers and the classroom environment will compete with you for influence. The school environment may or may not promote the calm and compassionate values you espouse. In the culture of American children, it is quite common that mock toughness, suggestive and provocative dress and behavior, and threatening language are the norm. Some children and teens go way beyond mere exclusion of those who are not "cool," to outright bullying and mental cruelty.

Most of us will encounter teasing, bullying, or lack of sympathy at some point, but it can severely decrease children's confidence and self-understanding if they are exposed to regular doses of it while still in their formative years. Less apparent than bullying, but also harmful, is the subtle pressure to conform to the group that exists when teachers do not know how to help children appreciate each other's individuality.

Although recent school reform has been focused mostly on academics, problems with bullying both at school and online continue. Only a tiny portion of the threats and small cruelties students visit on each other make the news. We cannot pretend that bad behavior is confined to children from dysfunctional or criminal homes. Several years ago in one American city, some boys on the football team got in trouble because they showed in class a video they had made of themselves torturing a cat. (I don't know where the teacher was.) Their coach was quoted as saying, "Too much is being made of this. We're not talking about a human being here."

There is the crux of the matter. If the adults in the school do not have sympathy and empathy for life and do not understand the danger of hardened hearts, how can the children? It is the teacher and his or her character, warmth, personality, intelligence, and dedication that sets the tone of the classroom and determines whether the classroom environment will be calm and supportive or sarcastic and undermining. Most children spend more than six hours a day in the classroom with their teachers providing leadership—for good or ill. This may be more waking hours than they spend with their parents, except on the weekends. Even the kindest and most well-intentioned teachers become harried by pressures such as crowded classrooms, neglected kids, parents who threaten lawsuits, and mandates to produce competent test-takers rather than competent human beings. High standards are a must, but academic learning does not, and should not, have to take precedence over learning to be a balanced human being.

In fact, learning is much, much easier for children when the schools and teachers create a culture in which students are respected and respectful, where feelings matter, where children's spiritual and natural needs are addressed, and where individual differences are celebrated. If a child is anxious because he doesn't know who is going to threaten or tease him at recess, how can he focus on fractions or writing a topic sentence? That sort of environment is no less harmful for the children who *are* in the popular groups that wield the power. Even kind children can get caught up in the attitude of "We're better than they are; stay cool lest you slip into the outcast group."

Public schools cannot help but reflect their society, and as long as we allow children to be victims of corporate greed, which sees them only as a market, the schools will not reflect calmness and compassion. However, in almost every setting you can find individual teachers who are loving and wise and who somehow survive in the system. It is your job as a parent to seek out the schools and teachers that promote your values. Look for schools that feel calm and relaxed; too many pay lip service to building character, but cannot actually implement their goal. Are children playing happily on the playground, or is there tension in many of their faces? Do children speak respectfully to each other in the classroom? It doesn't matter as much that they are collecting for the food bank as that they are respectful of all the individuals in the class. Compassionate action must begin at home.

If your child is miserable at school, go to school for a whole day and observe what is going on. Sometimes you need to change the way you are parenting or your child may need extra help, such as a tutor to help with academics or a therapist to help with adjustment difficulties. However, in many cases, it is the school that has the problem, not the child. Sometimes sensitive children are desperately unhappy because they are in a situation unsupportive of or even hostile to the values their families espouse. In your child's classroom, are children harmoniously and happily concentrating on tasks for the most part, or is there a sense of tension and fear? Overcrowded classrooms and a dehumanized system that makes test scores the highest priority make it difficult for even great teachers to be effective. The teacher may be trying to cope with a very difficult job without the people management skills and the support that she needs.

If the school environment is breaking your children's spirit and enthusiasm and teaching them the wrong values, do not think your children must conform to the broken system. If you can find or form small alternative schools that will attract families with values similar to yours, your children may be better off. However, even well-intentioned alternatives sometimes fail because of the lack of training and experience available to the teachers or the lack of leadership from the principal. Some parents find that homeschooling is the best answer, at least for a while.

I have learned from observing many children that one size does not fit all. Some children learn well in one situation and not in another. Many students thrive in Education for Life schools, with their emphasis on self-understanding and calm compassion. Some do well in Waldorf, with its emphasis on the arts. Other children, especially athletic ones, enjoy the advantages of a public school that offers them a chance to shine. I know some young people who have homeschooled, *plus* attended both public and private schools—all three! They benefited from each experience.

It is good that many parents no longer feel bound to a particular form of education, but are willing to look for the right fit at the right time for their children—recognizing that their needs could change.

not hothouse flowers

Sometimes parents ask about Living Wisdom School students: "When these children get out in the 'real world' won't they be too sensitive and soft to cope?"

I understand their concern; our setting *is* different from many other schools and workplaces. Influences of media and the corporate consumer culture are limited. Children are respected and taught to respect and cooperate with each other. The highest ideals of living, such as kindness, generosity, and aspiration (doing one's best), are emphasized. It is hard to imagine that learning in such an environment is a bad thing, and we know from experience that it works.

One of our graduates, when asked the difference between his Living Wisdom education and that of the other kids he encountered in a public high school, thoughtfully answered, "I noticed that the attitude of the other kids in my high school was 'What is the least I can do and get by?' At Living Wisdom, we were eager to do our best in everything."

Overstimulated and out-of-control children and teens naturally have trouble focusing their energies to do their best; calm and centered children easily direct their willpower and focus.

When children are educated in this way, they learn self-understanding and confidence in themselves. We have found that when they go on to public and private high schools they do not get caught up in playing the popularity game; they choose their peer groups carefully, and they thrive in the areas they choose to pursue. Far from being fragile, they have inner strength and determination.

They gravitate to friends and groups that support them, not worrying much about being popular or cool. Living Wisdom School students have graduated as valedictorians of public high school; graduated with honors from private boarding schools and public and private universities; and become lawyers, computer science engineers, administrators of non-profits, a computer animator, parents, firemen, a violin teacher, a chef, and a professional snowboarder who later became an archeologist. And that is just a few of them! I share all of this not to say "Look how great *our* students are" but rather to show what is possible. With like-minded parents and teachers, you can create cultures and schools that nourish your children in every way.

One of my former students, Gita McGilloway, who is getting a master's degree in management of non-profits, said this about her fellow graduates: "Each of my friends from Living Wisdom School shares two major things in common: a strong sense of self and an interest in giving back to the world." Giving children a childhood protected from the influences that take away their calmness and compassion produces not fragile adults, but adults with well-integrated personalities.

If you are a gardener, you know that a seedling given optimum conditions will grow into a strong plant, able to withstand the stresses of drought, heat, disease, and pests. However, a seedling that is stressed by irregular water or lack of food or light may survive, but as an adult plant it will never be as vigorous as the plant that the healthy seedling will become. In the same way, children who are exposed to the stresses of negative peer pressure, media saturation, and lack of compassion will have a more difficult time withstanding stresses later on than children who have the opportunity to develop in environments that are mentally and emotionally healthy.

The challenge, then, is
clear. Children thrive on an
experiential approach to values.
All they need is the help of a
caring, sensitive adult.

—Michael Nitai Deranja,
For Goodness' Sake

CHAPTER TWELVE

Becoming Calm and Compassionate Adults

FIONNA SAT IN MY OFFICE one sunny day in October 2001. Her son Keith was in our second grade class. Fionna's face was drawn and her crossed leg was swinging jerkily.

"Keith is just so upset by September 11. He can't sleep well, and he is anxious about more attacks." Her voice broke. "I'm just so worried about him."

And I'm worried about you, I thought. I asked her, "Has he seen the TV footage? How does he know about it?"

"Oh, you know, he hears talk about it," Fionna said.

"Maybe you could lie down with him at bedtime and listen to soothing music with him," I said. "And I have a CD of children's guided visualizations that would be great for you to listen to together." (See appendix 4 for details.)

Music and visualizations *would* calm Keith's fears, but I was hoping that they would also help his mother. It seemed to me that her fears and anxieties were so great that he had "caught them," just as one can catch a virus. Children easily pick up on their parents' moods because they are emotionally connected to the significant adults in their world. Carla Hannaford writes in *Awakening the Child Heart*, "As adults, we can't provide the peace and security required in order to develop the child heart in children if we are in frequent stress, for children pick up our stress like sponges."

When parents are relaxed and calm about a situation, children follow their lead. When a parent is uptight and anxious, a child, even though he may not have an inkling of why the parent is worried, will pick right up on that energy. Sometimes the parent will project the problem as being the child's when it actually originates with the parent.

We teachers experience this often! Sometimes the class seems happy, cooperative, and busily engaged. Other times the same children are whiny, unwilling, and unfocused. Every good teacher eventually realizes that on the days that she herself is calmly energetic, organized, and cheerful, the children usually are too. On the days that she is low-energy, irritable, and moody—lo and behold, the children are mirrors reflecting her state of mind!

The year before I began teaching in a Living Wisdom School, I was a librarian in a public elementary school. It was an amazing experience: I learned more that year than any other in my career because I got to observe how the varied teaching styles of twenty-one different teachers affected their classes. One first grade teacher had a very outgoing, gregarious personality; her class was rowdy, happy, and easygoing. Another first grade teacher was imaginative, humble, and dedicated. She *never* raised her voice and often whispered to her children. Her class was quiet and receptive—they treated the library almost like a temple.

I remember two third grade classes in particular. One teacher was a loving, relaxed young woman who laughed easily. Her children would come into the library asking for the latest book she was reading aloud to them. Whatever the book, they thought it was "the best book they ever heard," as they reflected her enthusiasm. Her children adored her.

I dreaded the arrival of the other third grade class. There were undercurrents of dissatisfaction and bullying in this class. When I finally had an occasion to spend a few minutes in this teacher's classroom, I understood. Had I not actually witnessed her classroom management style, I would not have suspected that she ruled with sarcasm and fault-finding. She derided children who were not on task, in a scornful tone of voice. It was obvious she had favorites, and that some children were not ever going to gain her favor. I learned that it was not so much the different classes of children that had particular characteristics as it was their particular *teachers*. The children in their charge reflected their personalities to a considerable degree.

becoming calm and compassionate yourself

We, as teachers and parents, set the tone for our children to be calm and compassionate. Tobin Hart puts it beautifully in *The Secret Spiritual World of Children*: "The language we speak, the mood of our home, a gentle meal, a sane pace, an unconditional tone in our voice, the right music, or a candle or flower at the dinner table all can balance toughness and excitement with tenderness. Tenderness makes it safe for the heart to rise to the surface."

Being a good model is, of course, the best way to teach children. On the other hand, you can teach your child patience and self-control even if you have not yet perfectly mastered them yourself. Just as you do not need to know calculus to help your child with long division, you do not have to be a saint to help your child learn the fundamentals of love and peace. As long as we are honest with children and admit our failures and genuinely regret them, children can overlook our shortcomings. In fact, they often teach us by their love and forgiveness.

One morning I was sitting at my desk in my fourth grade classroom busily getting materials ready for the day as children arrived. Kids had been asking me questions, and I had been responding, but I was not greeting each one with full attention. Suddenly, I felt little arms around me and a sweet kiss on my cheek. I smiled broadly as I hugged Tabitha back.

She said, "You looked like you needed that!"

I was chastened. I realized immediately (as embarrassed as I am to admit it) that I had not been making eye contact with the children. A nine-year-old had realized that my grumpiness had nothing to do with her, and that a little love would help a lot! I resolved to be more "present" for the children, not letting my anxiety about getting everything done take me out of the heart. I had just experienced a great model of how I could help children who were having a hard time. So often when children are unruly or uncooperative, we correct them verbally; we lecture them; we explain why. And really what is needed is a hug! A little human contact, love, and understanding can often help us release the tension we're holding and relax into peace.

How can we as adults become more calm and compassionate? The suggestions for your children in the first eleven chapters will be helpful for you as well: pets, nature, slow music, body work, and high-mindedness are not only for children! In this chapter, I will share four further techniques:

- Taking a breath
- Meditation or centering prayer
- Letting love flow
- Looking for strengths

These practices will help improve your ability to be inwardly calm and able to mentally step back from a situation to ask yourself, "What is the best thing I can do to help this child right now?"

taking a breath

Deep breathing is a great technique to calm yourself when you feel angry or impatient. Taking long, slow breaths may sound too simplistic to be of value, but controlling the breath is a very effective technique to calm the emotions and the heart rate. Dr. Andrew Weil, in an interview on National Public Radio, said the most important piece of health advice he could give is "Learn to breathe!" The interviewer laughed, but Dr. Weil was serious.

Many mothers learn about the benefits of conscious breathing during pregnancy and childbirth. Most childbirth preparation classes teach controlled breathing to relieve stress and tension and even to regulate the blood flow to the unborn baby. A busy mother may wonder when she could possibly find time for it, but those who take time for this practice wonder how they coped before they learned how. Victoria, a member of my spiritual parenting group and the busy mother of a baby and a toddler, says,

> *I couldn't live without "breathing through" difficult times when the kids are both fussing. It helps me stay centered to turn inward for a few moments and focus on deep breaths. After that I am able to more effectively help my children calm down. I simply wouldn't have been able to get them recentered if I hadn't taken some time (even as little as three seconds) to center myself.*
>
> *I find that it makes all the difference between snapping at my children in a harried moment and being able to find an effective or creative solution to whatever they might be upset about. All I do is very slowly breathe in and out two to five times while reminding myself that I can stay calm even when my children cannot.*

If you have never taken a yoga or breath-work class, you may not know how to breathe from the diaphragm. Lie down on your back and take a few slow breaths. Put your hands on either side of your rib cage with the fingertips on your stomach an inch or two apart. When you inhale, do your hands and fingers expand outward? If not, to practice expanding your diaphragm, use the muscles around your abdomen to push your fingers outward as you inhale. I recommend you try a yoga class or martial arts or tai chi. These classes will help you get in touch with your breath and with how it feels to calm your emotions through physical discipline. Once you understand it, you can help your children learn it too (see chapter 7).

meditation or centering prayer

You have probably heard about the benefits of meditation and the studies that have shown it decreases blood pressure, helps the immune system, and more. *Time* magazine featured a cover article titled "The Science of Meditation" in August 2003. Stress causes us to be restless and impatient; meditation can help reduce that stress and help you to stay calm in the hustle and bustle of your life. In appendix 4, I recommend a book that will help you learn to meditate. If you can find a teacher and group who meditate together, that is an excellent way to learn.

If you prefer a Christian approach, you can learn Centering Prayer, developed by Father Thomas Keating (see appendix 4). Christian groups have formed all around the country to practice Centering Prayer together; call churches in your area and ask if they know of a group, and check the Contemplative Outreach website to find out more.

Meditation enables you to get perspective on your life and your children—by *not* thinking about them. It is paradoxical, but it works this way: it is as if you have a well of inner peace that you can drink from. Learning to operate the pump is not easy; it does take willpower and practice. It is the way to find your own calmness and compassion so that your actions are more in harmony with the high ideals you have for yourself and your children.

letting love flow

All healthy parents love their children. When you visualize the love you feel as being an expression of divine unconditional love that you are tuning in to, it becomes less personal to you and helps you expand your awareness. We learn that love is always there to be received and given; the capacity to love is not original with you, and your child's future happiness is not solely dependent on you! It is paradoxical that being more impersonal helps you love more.

Some teachers advise us to see ourselves not as the doers, but as instruments through which divine energy flows. This advice works well in our interactions with children. At first, it may be only at the harmonious times that you remember to do this. It is easy to imagine God's love flowing through you to your child when he is being adorable. Next, you can begin to call on that love and guidance in the more challenging times.

Instead of reacting automatically when a child misbehaves or defies you, you can pause, and ask for unconditional love and wisdom to flow *through* you to the child. When children are being what we perceive as "difficult," if we stop, take a breath, and mentally give the child love, we will instantly see the cause of their misbehavior or mood and be able to help them. Often the solution that comes to you is not the first reactive thought you had. When we are focused on giving the child what she needs rather than on how she is obstructing our own expectations, the outcome is always better. What she needs might be a no—but "*No*" said with even-mindedness feels quite different from "*No!*" said with frustration.

Parents identify strongly with their children, sometimes ignoring the child's individual personality and inclinations. As parents and teachers we can influence our children, but we cannot control them. In the long run, it will help you to accept that although you are your child's guide, protector, and greatest influence, your child is ultimately his or her own self. As Michael Deranja, codirector of the Education for Life Foundation, once said, "You can't force a tomato seed to grow up to be a cucumber!"

When my stepson was about twelve or thirteen years old, he was in some sort of minor trouble. His dad and I had sat him down for a serious talk, and he suddenly blurted, "You just want me to be your *perfect* little boy because you're both teachers and you don't want me to embarrass you!"

His claim was so heartfelt; it stopped me cold. I thought, *Well, yes, of course I want you to be our perfect boy; why wouldn't I?* And I realized what a burden that was for him, and that I needed to give him more love and fewer judgments. Once I had less attachment to the outcome, he even began to listen to my opinions. Our relationship grew more harmonious and deeper as I shifted my view of my role from one who should teach him to attain a certain ideal to one who would love him for who he was, helping him to his next step of growth.

Parents tend to be either strict and threatened by negotiation and compromise or permissive and unable to establish consistent boundaries. It is not easy to strike a balance between providing our children with the environment and guidance that enables them to be the best they can be and simply relaxing into acceptance and affection for who they presently are. It helps to remind yourself that your children's future is not solely up to you. Each child has his or her own qualities at birth—before our input even starts— and a set of life circumstances that you influence, but do not control.

looking for strengths

Recognizing and providing opportunities for inspiring children to take their next step in maturity, rather than chiding them about their shortcomings, is a tenet of the calm and compassionate approach.

I once heard Dorothy Briggs speak, and I never forgot her admonition: "It takes ten warm fuzzies for one cold prickly to be heard!" Warm fuzzies are compliments and positive feedback, and cold pricklies are corrections or reprimands.

Many times over the years I have had a student whose behavior was so distracting to the rest of the class that before I knew it I'd be saying multiple times, "Sit down.

Don't interrupt. Please wait your turn to speak." It is easy to get through the whole day with a child and realize you have not given even one warm fuzzy, such as "That's an important perspective; I appreciate your contribution" or "Thank you for shutting the door; that was helpful."

The good parent or teacher is always on the lookout for successes—moments where the behavior is on track—and gives positive feedback. This will not change all of the child's annoying behaviors, but it helps establish a rapport and a relationship in which the child feels respected enough to listen when you do have to correct him.

The ability to give positive feedback is an important skill for parents and teachers. But it can be taken to a deeper level. Even more powerful is the ability to understand the child's true nature and to reflect it back with affirmation and approval. Parents sometimes do not see who a child really is because their vision is so clouded by who they want that child to be.

A young mother told me, after her child had attended preschool and kindergarten at my school, that our parent classes and our teachers had not only helped her with parenting, but had "transformed" her relationship with her daughter.

"How was that?!" I asked.

"You helped me to see and focus on my daughter's gifts and strengths. Before, I had been so focused on helping her improve what I saw as her weak points, that I had lost sight of her special talents."

Respect for a child's nature can be taken to a level that transcends personal tendencies, emotions, and thoughts.

Children need adults in their lives who believe in their capacity to be courageous, loving, calm, and compassionate human beings. "This does not mean playing Pollyanna or closing our eyes to wrong behavior," Eknath Easwaran writes in *Original Goodness*. "It means simply that we will never lose faith in any person's capacity to change. Without that faith people lose faith in themselves, and without faith in yourself it is not possible to improve."

It is not complicated to nurture children's calmness and compassion, but that doesn't mean it is easy. Changing our attitudes and our approach to anything can be challenging, but you have already begun. Just by reading this book, you have already put out the intention to be more conscious of your impact on the spirit of the children in your life.

Although the topic is serious, the approach can be light! Play with your children, not only in games and activities you choose, but also following their lead. Nothing will relax you more—or help you understand your children better— than playing with them. As you get to know them better by entering their reality, you will discover ways you can gently guide them in their growth as compassionate human beings.

Your children *can* be active but calm, and they have tremendous capacity within for heartfelt compassion. They are blessed by having you in their life as you learn together how to become balanced and joyful. Your intention to nurture their greatest potential helps them realize an expansive future, filled with possibilities we can barely imagine.

Afterword

I AM INTERESTED to hear about your experiences in using the practical steps at the ends of chapters 1 to 10. You can contact me at my website www.susandermond.com where you will find photos and more on related topics.

Calm and Compassionate
Self-Inventory for Parents

Rate yourself on a scale of 0 to 3.

    0 Never
    1 Once in a while
    2 Fairly often
    3 Consistently

___ My child and I look for beauty in our surroundings and kindness in people and acknowledge them. (See chapter 5.)

___ Our schedule allows for some downtime for my children and time for us to hang out together, talk, and share books, games, and outings into nature. (See the introduction and chapter 11.)

___ I help my child expand his awareness outside of himself to the needs of others by giving him opportunities to relate with pets, younger children, and nature. (See chapters 2 and 4.)

___ My child has daily quiet time when no media is turned on and (ideally) when he can be alone to fantasize, be creative, and just learn to be with himself. (See chapter 9.)

___ If we see an injured bird or animal, my child and I take care of it, move it to safety, or mentally bless it. We take spiders outside and release them or relocate them to plants. (See chapters 2 and 10.)

___ I do not allow my child or her playmate to call other children names or use put-down words, such as *stupid, dumb, fat,* or *clumsy.* (See chapters 10 and 11.)

___ I am involved in my child's school; I have observed recess and in the classroom, and I am aware of the influence of my child's teacher and peers. (See chapter 11.)

____ If my child has trouble sleeping, I help him relax through warm baths, foot rubs, and humming or playing soothing music. (See chapters 6 and 7.)

____ Our family has daily routines and seasonal rituals that convey a sense of continuity and help our children feel calm and secure. (See chapter 1.)

____ My children get vigorous exercise—running, swinging, biking, playing ball—for at least an hour a day. (See chapter 7.)

____ When my child is overexcited—talking fast, jumping up and down, or gasping for breath—I touch her calmly and ask her to take two or three long slow breaths and speak normally. I breathe with her and consciously relax my own body so my touch is calming. (See chapters 7 and 12.)

____ I read aloud to my children books in which some characters have heart-centered qualities and a tone that is not sarcastic, but sincere. (See chapter 3.)

____ I provide opportunities for my child to concentrate and focus for fun, through games and mental challenges. (See chapter 8.)

____ My child eats healthy food, drinks water rather than sodas or too much juice, and gets plenty of sleep. (See chapter 11.)

____ I look for opportunities to help my child develop her own power to help others; for example, asking her to hold the door for an older person rather than doing it myself, or noticing when she does something helpful unasked. (See chapter 10.)

____ My child listens only to age-appropriate music, and watches no more than three hours of TV or DVDs weekly. (See chapter 11.)

____ I practice patience, deep breathing, and lovingness as I wait for my children to get out of the car, walk up and down steps, or tell me a lengthy story about what happened. If I need to cut the story short, I do it respectfully, as I would to another adult. (See chapters 11 and 12.)

____ I observe which of my child's playmates have a positive influence on my child's calmness and which do not. I notice my child's mood and contentment level after play dates and do my best to facilitate calming relationships. (See chapter 11.)

____ When my children misbehave, rather than reacting, I take deep breaths and stay calm and impersonal as I correct them. (See chapter 12.)

____ My own calmness and compassion is a high priority for me, and I make time for the spiritual practices, friendships, and health measures that support my inner peace. (See chapter 12.)

What Is Your Score?

Add all your ratings and get one total. If your score is

45–60: You are doing an amazing job to help your children to be calm and compassionate. You should be giving workshops or coordinating a parent group!

35–44: You are conscious of the importance of creating a calm and compassionate home. It will be a natural flow for you to do more activities from the book. Expand your boundaries by choosing practical steps from an area that you have never considered before and notice their effect.

20–34: Some of these concepts may be new to you, but you can begin to practice more of them to help your children calm down and expand their awareness outside of themselves. Go through the practical steps sections and highlight the activities that appeal to you. Or go back through the self-inventory and look at the actions that you rated 0 or 1. Choose one new calm and compassionate practice that appeals to you to experiment with for a week, and observe the results. What do you notice about the effects on both you and your kids? If your children are not receptive at the time you choose, drop it and wait for the right moment. It will take a while for everyone to get headed in a new direction!

0–19: Choose activities from whichever chapter you feel most in tune with and begin trying the practical steps from that chapter. You will see an improvement as you begin to implement some of these recommendations. Be gentle and subtle in adding new elements to your life.

It might seem overwhelming to you to go too fast, and your children will probably rebel if you do. Do not emphasize what you are changing or getting rid of in your children's life; if you do, your family may feel threatened. You may be stressed and need personal support; find parents with whom you can share your hopes and frustrations. If you do not have neighbors or other parents of your child's peers to befriend, find a group through a church, environmental group, Moms or Dads Club, or yoga class.

Self-Inventory for Teachers

Rate yourself on a scale of 0 to 3.

    0 Never
    1 Once in a while
    2 Fairly often
    3 Consistently

___ I play calming music (45 to 60 beats per minute) during transitions and silent work periods, and when the class is restless. (See chapter 6.)

___ In my classroom acts of compassion are recognized; for example, with a verbal acknowledgment or an appreciative smile. (See chapter 11.)

___ When children are restless and unable to pay attention, I have them drink water and give them a chance to move in a controlled way, such as doing the "Hokey Pokey," "Simon Says" with no one ever out, or clapping patterns. (See chapter 7.)

___ I give the class avenues to *experience* compassion for each other; for example, writing sympathy notes if someone's pet dies, or fetching a bandage for someone's cut or scrape. (See the introduction and chapter 10.)

___ I give the class opportunities to expand their awareness to younger children in the school and to animals. Possibilities include reading partners, secret gifts or holiday treats, inviting younger classes to class presentations, and pet visits. (See chapters 4 and 10.)

___ I am developing a repertoire of mental and physical challenges to help children focus their attention. (See chapter 8.)

___ I make the emotional relaxation necessary for learning a priority. I stop class to address individual needs, to give reassurance when needed or to help problem-solve a little difficulty such as not having a pencil. I show compassion to individuals who may be having a bad day; for example, by giving them a stuffie to hold, a note saying I care, or a touch and eye contact, with the words, "I can see it's rough for you today; just do your best." (See chapters 11 and 12.)

___ The class has daily rituals—such as singing before meals, calendar time, circle time, sharing time, a thought for the day, special music when returning from recess—to help keep children grounded and give them opportunities to "come back to center." (See chapter 1.)

___ I do my best to show love for the inner potential of a child even if I have to set firm boundaries or reprimand her behavior. (See chapters 11 and 12.)

___ I have personal rituals and routines that I use daily to stay calm and loving in the midst of the chaos of the classroom; for example, deep breathing, listening to calming music, doing tai chi or yoga, or talking to a colleague. (See chapter 12.)

___ I teach my students how to breathe diaphragmatically, and we practice it to get ready for a test or public performances. (See chapters 7 and 12.)

___ Daily I bring uplifting and generous thoughts, photos, stories, and special objects into the classroom to share, and I invite the children to "notice" beautiful moments. (See chapter 5.)

___ The classroom environment is supportive and orderly, giving children the space to relax and create. There are periods of silence in which children can process information and input. (See chapters 9 and 11.)

___ I choose read-alouds that touch children's hearts, depict compassionate actions, and portray characters with self-control and ethics. (See chapter 3.)

___ I listen to my children's thoughts and pay attention to their feelings. I seek awareness of the next step of growth for each individual, rather than projecting my own needs and desires onto them. (See chapters 10 and 12.)

What Is Your Score?

Add all your ratings and get one total.

35-45: You are doing an amazing job to create a calm and compassionate classroom.

25-34: You are conscious of the importance of creating a calm and compassionate classroom; you will find that adding more activities from the book flows naturally.

10-24: Some of these concepts may be new to you, but you can begin to add more of them to make yours a calmer and more compassionate classroom. Go back and look at the ones that you rated 0 or 1. Choose a couple that appeal to you; try them both at least a couple of times this week and observe the results. What do you notice? Is this one that you can do to help your children? Taking a yoga, tai chi, or meditation class may help you.

0-9: You probably need support. Meet regularly with a teacher you perceive to be capable and compassionate to discuss your efforts. Try one new calm and compassionate practice a week. Implement it once a day if possible. Keep a journal of what you observe. Your classroom will begin to change, and you will find more satisfaction in teaching.

Recommended Read-Alouds

There are many, good picture books out there to choose from. These are just a few of my favorites.

picture books for the young (ages 3 to 9) and young at heart

Baylor, Byrd. *I'm in Charge of Celebrations*. Illus. by Peter Parnall. New York: Scribner's, 1986. Celebrating the cycles of nature and the joy and mystery of all life.

Berger, Barbara. *A Lot of Otters*. New York: Philomel Books, 1997. Beautiful and expansive. Kids love these pictures.

Bowen, Connie. *I Believe in Me*. Unity Village, MO: Unity, 1995. A lyrical book that affirms the best in each of us.

Cannon, Janell. *Stellaluna*. New York: Scholastic, 1993. The little bat, Stellaluna, learns to appreciate differences.

Curtis, Chara. *All I See Is Part of Me*. Bellevue, WA: Illumination Arts, 1994. Already a quiet classic among those who believe in the interconnectedness of all creation.

Dunbar, Joyce. *A Chick Called Saturday*. Illus. by Brita Granstrom. Grand Rapids, MI: Eerdmans Books for Young Readers, 2003. Saturday cannot swim like a duck or honk like a goose. But just wait until he finds out what he can do!

Fyleman, Rose. *A Fairy Went A-Marketing*. Illus. by Jamichael Henterly. New York: Dutton, 1986. A quiet story about a fairy who collects treasures of nature, then sets them free. A classic.

Lobel, Arnold. *Frog and Toad Are Friends. Frog and Toad Together*. New York: Harper and Row, 1970 and 1971.Endearing episodes from the lives of two close friends.

Reed-Jones, Carol. *The Tree in the Ancient Forest.* Illus. by Christopher Canyon. Nevada City, CA: Dawn, 1995. The interdependence of plant and animal life in an old-growth forest is the theme, beautifully illustrated.

Ryan, Pam Munoz. *One Hundred Is a Family.* New York: Hyperion, 1994. A counting book with a message: we are all one human family.

Santangelo, Colony Elliott. *Brother Wolf of Gubbio.* New York: Handprint Books, 2000. A realistic version of the Saint Francis legend, with inspiring artwork.

Seligson, Susan. *Amos, the Story of an Old Dog and His Couch.* New York: Little, Brown, 1987. Not every child likes every book, but I have yet to find a child who didn't giggle at this one. Rollicking good fun.

Tickle, Phyllis. *This Is What I Pray Today.* New York: Penguin, 2007. Offers Jewish, Christian, and Muslim children's prayers for different times of day. Many based on Psalms.

Tutu, Archibishop Desmond. *God's Dream.* Philadelphia: Quaker Books, 2008. We are brothers and sisters, no matter our color or way of worship.

Varley, Susan. *Badger's Parting Gifts.* New York: Lothrop, Lee and Shepard Books, 1984. Badger's friends are sad at his death but realize he left them with beautiful memories and love.

Wood, Douglas. *Granddad's Prayers of the Earth.* Cambridge, MA: Candlewick Press, 1999. Prayer is not only asking for things, but also being present with gratitude or joy.

chapter books and picture book biographies

These are great stories that are timeless in their relevance and meaning.

FOR AGES 7 TO 10

Around second, third, or fourth grade, children are ready for more text and more information. Yet, they are still emotionally young. These books honor both aspects of the maturing child.

Fritz, Jean. *What's the Big Idea, Ben Franklin?* Illus. by Margot
Tomes. New York: Putnam, 1976. A very entertaining account of
Franklin's life and accomplishments.

Le Guin, Ursula. *Catwings*. New York: Scholastic, 1988. Short little
fantasy of cats who fly. Children love it, and it's the first of three.

Ryan, Pam Munoz. *When Marian Sang*. Illus. by Brian Selznick. New
York: Scholastic, 2002. The life of Marian Anderson rendered in
gorgeous illustrations with a deeply felt text.

Rylant, Cynthia. *Thimbleberry Stories*. Orlando, FL: Harcourt, 2000.
Four sweetly illustrated stories about Nigel Chipmunk and his
friendships. These stories bring compassion and unselfishness to
life in young minds.

Stanley, Melanie Zucker. *George Washington Carver*. Glen Allen,
VA: Foxhound Publishing, 2000. Everyone should spend some
time with this great man; the book is illustrated entirely with
photographs.

Wilder, Laura Ingalls. *Little House in the Big Woods* and the rest of
the series. New York: HarperCollins. Wholesome and based on
fact. Although the characters are all sisters, the father is a great
role model for boys.

.... FOR AGES 8 TO 12 ....

Barron, T. A. *The Lost Years of Merlin*. New York: Philomel, 1996.
First of a series beloved by many.

Burnford, Shelia. *The Incredible Journey*. New York: Bantam, 1990.
Three pets travel hundreds of miles by themselves to find their
family.

Clements, Andrew. *Frindle*. Illus. by Brian Selznick. New York:
Simon and Schuster, 1996. In this unusual story, Nate's teacher
teaches him not only to love words, but also to use his willpower.

Coville, Bruce. *Jeremy Thatcher, Dragon Hatcher*. San Diego:
Harcourt, 2002. A matchless read-aloud, this story combines the
ever-popular dragon theme with a realistic contemporary story.
Short chapters and lots of suspense. Jeremy learns to expand his
sympathies and to see his little dragon as a real being, not merely
his possession.

DiCamillo, Kate. *The Tale of Despereaux*. Cambridge, MA: Candlewick Press, 2003. The adventures of the endearing mouse, Despereaux. Surrounded by small-minded mice, he dares to follows his heart. A sweet tale of the triumph of love and sincerity over meanness of the heart.

King-Smith, Dick. *Babe, the Gallant Pig*. New York: Knopf, 2005. The movie is good, but the book is glorious. Sweet and touching.

Lewis, C. S. *The Lion, the Witch and the Wardrobe*. New York: HarperCollins, 2000. A beloved classic and the first of the Chronicles of Narnia.

Rawls, Wilson. *Summer of the Monkeys*. New York: Bantam Doubleday, 1999. A boy in the Ozarks attempts to catch monkeys that have escaped from a circus train. A hilarious story, filled with strong values.

Speare, Elizabeth George. *The Sign of the Beaver*. Boston: Houghton Mifflin, 1983. A young boy on the frontier of Colonial America makes friends with a Native American child and takes care of the homestead while his parents are away.

.... FOR AGES 10 TO 13 ....

Brown, Tom, Jr. *The Tracker: The True Story of Tom Brown, Jr.* New York: Berkley Books, 1979. Nonfiction. The story of two boys growing up in the New Jersey pine barrens with an Apache grandfather who teaches them survival skills.

Furlong, Monica. *Wise Child*. New York: Knopf, 1987. An orphaned child who doesn't fit in, Wise Child finds her true calling apprenticing with Juniper, the village healer. This book rates number one with girls from ten years old to adults.

Montgomery, L. M. *Anne of Green Gables*. Toronto: Tundra Books, 2000. Irrepressible Anne, an eleven-year-old orphan, is sent by mistake to live with a middle-aged brother and sister on a Prince Edward Island farm and embraces her new life. Beloved by generations of girls.

Naylor, Phyllis Reynolds. *Shiloh*. New York: Atheneum, 1991. A Newberry-winning story about a boy and the abused dog he saves. Compassion, right and wrong, truth and falsehood— all are themes. Too harsh for the younger set.

Reid Banks, Lynn. *The Indian in the Cupboard.* Garden City, NY: Doubleday, 1980. A British boy learns empathy from an action figure!

Stanger, Margaret. *That Quail, Robert.* New York: HarperPerennial, 1992. A sweet and true account of Stanger's pet quail. Animal lovers and older children usually love it.

Voigt, Cynthia. *Homecoming.* New York: Simon Pulse, 2002. Abandoned by their mentally ill mother, four children make their way from New Jersey to their unknown grandmother on the Chesapeake Bay. No more resourceful or introspective character exists in children's literature than the older sister, Dicey. First of a series.

books for young teens

Some of these, such as *The December Rose* and *Little Britches*, are great introductory read-alouds. Others, such as *The Sword in the Stone*, have long descriptive passages and are for experienced listeners. All are wonderful for the child who is an avid reader, herself.

FOR AGES 12 TO 15

Brown, Tom, Jr. *The Vision.* New York: Berkley Books, 1979. *The Tracker* describes the outward training; this book tells us about the transcendental experiences that living in nature brought these two boys.

Fletcher, Susan. *Shadow Spinner.* New York: Atheneum, 1998. Marjan, a thirteen-year-old crippled girl, joins the Sultan's harem in ancient Persia and gathers stories for Shahrazad.

Garfield, Leon. *The December Rose.* New York: Viking Kestrel, 1987. Barnaby, a London chimney sweep, survives by his wits, but learns about family love from an unlikely trio of Thames boaters. Humorous, but also full of danger and suspense.

McCaffrey, Anne. *Dragonsong.* New York: Aladdin, 1976. Can a girl be a dragonsinger? Menolly proves her talent both in music and in empathy with dragonlike lizards. *Dragonsinger and Dragondrums* follow in this Harper Hall trilogy.

Moody, Ralph. *Little Britches.* Lincoln, NE: University of Nebraska Press, 1978. Growing up on the prairie, Little Britches wants his own horse. Amusing, sad, and outrageous incidents abound, just like in real life. The integrity of his parents only gets stronger for the hardships they endure and will endear them to every reader. A bit sexist in the roles of the brother and sister, but the book reflects the times it portrays.

Speare, Elizabeth George. *The Bronze Bow.* Boston: Houghton Mifflin, 1989. Set in the Holy Land at the time of Christ, with older teens as the main characters.

Staples, Suzanne Fisher. *Shiva's Fire.* New York: Farrar Straus Giroux, 2000. The story of a Hindu Indian girl who struggles with her widowed mother to survive and to express her musical gifts. Staples excels in writing about girls and young women in other cultures.

Staples, Suzanne Fisher. *Shabanu.* New York: Knopf, 1991. The life of a Muslim desert girl and her nomad family is close and loving, but danger threatens to destroy their future.

White, T. H. *The Sword in the Stone.* New York: Philomel, 1993. King Arthur's childhood and the magical education Merlin gave him.

Recommended Resources

These resources are for those who might want to pursue further concepts and activities that were mentioned in the text. They all support in some way the development of calm and compassionate children.

....
resources for both parents and educators
....

Sharing Nature with Children by Joseph Cornell (Nevada City, CA: Dawn, 1998).

Education for Life: Preparing Children to Meet the Challenges by J. Donald Walters (Nevada City, CA: Crystal Clarity, 1997).

Last Child in the Woods: Saving Our Children from Nature Deficit Disorder by Richard Louv (Chapel Hill, NC: Algonquin Books, 2005).

The Read-Aloud Handbook, 6th ed., by Jim Trelease (New York: Penguin, 2006).

Teaching Meditation to Children by David Fontana and Ingrid Slack (Rockport, MA: Element Books, 1998).

How to Meditate by John Novak (Nevada City, CA: Crystal Clarity, rev. 1992).

Contemplative Outreach website, www.centeringprayer.com. The organization dedicated to spreading the practice of Fr. Thomas Keating's centering prayer.

Affirmations for Self-Healing by J. Donald Walters (Nevada City, CA: Crystal Clarity, rev. 2005).

Education for Life website, www.edforlife.org. Information on the system and philosophy plus parent and teacher training.

other resources for parents

Easy to Love, Difficult to Discipline: The Seven Basic Skills for Turning Conflict into Cooperation by Becky Bailey (New York: William Morrow, 2000).

Busy but Balanced: Practical and Inspirational Ways to Create a Calmer, Closer Family by Mimi Doe (New York: St. Martin's Griffin, 2001).

Scary News: 12 Ways to Raise Joyful Children When the Headlines Are Full of Fear by Lorna Knox (Nevada City, CA: Crystal Clarity, 2004).

Everyday Blessings: The Inner Work of Mindful Parenting by Myla Kabbat-Zinn (New York: Hyperion, 1997).

Supporting Your Child's Inner Life by Toby Moorhouse, a visualizations CD (Nevada City, CA: Living Wisdom School, rev. 2006).

Living Simply with Children by Marie Sherlock (New York: Three Rivers Press, 2003).

other resources for educators

For Goodness' Sake: Helping Children and Teens Discover Life's Higher Values by Michael Nitai Deranja (Nevada City, CA: Crystal Clarity, 2004).

Conscious Discipline: 7 Basic Skills for Brain Smart Classroom Management, by Becky A. Bailey (Oviedo, FL: Loving Guidance, rev. 2001).

Smart Moves: Why Learning Is Not All in Your Head, 2nd. ed., by Carla Hannaford (Salt Lake City: Great River Books, 2005).

Win-Win Games for All Ages: Cooperative Activities for Building Social Skills by Sambhava and Josette Luvmour (Gabriola Island, BC: New Society Publishers, 2002).

Education for Life websites: www.edforlife.org; www.livingwisdomportland.org/teacher-training.htm.

music to calm and soothe

Relax: Meditations for Flute and Cello by Donald Walters (Nevada City: Crystal Clarity, 2003). My personal favorite. Cellist David Eby's playing melts away stress.

Secrets of Love: Melodies to Open Your Heart by Donald Walters (Nevada City: Crystal Clarity, 2000). Watch how your and your children's energy and thoughts change as you listen to these gentle instrumentals.

Music for Concentration by the Arcangelos Chamber Ensemble (Ogden, UT: ABT Music, 2003). Mostly Bach and Vivaldi; calming and uplifting.

Music for Accelerated Learning by Steven Halpern (Ashland, OR: Inner Peace Music, 1999).

Music for the Mozart Effect, Volume 2, *Heal the Body: Relax and Unwind* by Don Campbell (Spring Hill Music, 1998). Don Campbell has many Mozart Effect albums out. Be sure to get one specifically for relaxation; others may be more activating.

music to activate

Medicine Woman II by Medwyn Goodall (Ashland, OR: New World Music, 1998).

Week-End Classics: Sousa Marches by the Band of the Grenadier Guards (London: Decca, 1990).

Bach Brandenburg Concertos by Il Giardino Armonico (Hamburg: Teldec Classics, 1997). Concerto No. 2 in F major and Concerto No. 3 in G major, in particular. Just skip over the second, adagio movements.

A Gentle Wind Inc. website: www.gentlewind.com. Their selections include the highest caliber of themes and language. Go for the ones that have garnered numerous awards. A great source of lively music for children is *A Gentle Wind: Songs and Stories for Children.*

books, music, toys, games

Hearthsong, toys (Madison, VA). www.hearthsong.com.

Chinaberry, books and other treasures for the whole family (San Diego, CA). www.chinaberry.com.

Mindware, brainy games and toys (St. Paul, MN). www.mindware.com.

Magic Cabin, toys and more (Madison, VA). www.magiccabin.com.

Notes

·· INTRODUCTION ··

The Dalai Lama, *An Open Heart: Practicing Compassion in Everyday Life* (Boston: Little, Brown, 2001).

Michael Lerner, *Spirit Matters* (Charlottesville, VA: Hampton Roads, 2000).

Rolin McCraty, "The Resonant Heart," in *Shift: At the Frontiers of Consciousness*, December 2004.

·· PART ONE ··

Carla Hannaford, *Awakening the Child Heart* (Captain Cook, HI: Jamilla Nur, 2002).

Joseph Cornell, *Sharing Nature with Children* (Nevada City, CA: Dawn, 1998).

·· CHAPTER ONE ··

Becky A. Bailey, *Conscious Discipline: 7 Basic Skills for Brain Smart Classroom Management* (Oviedo, FL: Loving Guidance, rev. 2001).

Barbara Fiese, "A Review of 50 Years of Research on Naturally Occurring Family Routines and Rituals: Cause for Celebration," *Journal of Family Psychology*, Vol. 16, No. 4.

Donald Walters, "Go With Love," *I Came from Joy*, compact disc, 2003, Crystal Clarity.

·· CHAPTER TWO ··

Richard Louv, *Last Child in the Woods: Saving Our Children from Nature Deficit Disorder* (Chapel Hill, NC: Algonquin Books, 2005).

Joseph Cornell, *Sharing Nature with Children* (Nevada City, CA: Dawn, 1998).

Nancy Wells and Gary Evans, as quoted by Susan Lang, "A Green Scene Can Help Rural Children Endure Stress, Researchers Find," *Cornell Chronicle*, May 8, 2003. www.news.cornell.edu/Chronicle/03/5.8.03/nature_rural_stress.html.

Andrea Faber Taylor and Frances Kuo, quoted by Willow Lawson, "ADHD's Outdoor Cure," *Psychology Today*, March/April 2004. www.psychologytoday.com/articles/pto-20040406-000015.html.

Mel Bartholomew, *All New Square Foot Gardening* (Nashville: Cool Springs Press, 2005).

·· CHAPTER THREE ··

Anne Commire, ed. *Something about the Author*, vol. 62. Farmington Hills, MI: Gale Research, Inc., 1990. Patricia MacLachlan is the author of *Sarah, Plain and Tall* and many other books.

Peggy Jenkins, *The Joyful Child* (Tucson: Harbinger House, 1989).

Darlene L. Witte-Townsend, "Something from Nothing: Exploring Dimensions of Children's Knowing through the Repeated Reading of Favorite Books," in *International Journal of Children's Spirituality*, August 2004.

Carla Hannaford, *Smart Moves: Why Learning Is Not All in Your Head*, 2nd. ed. (Salt Lake City: Great River Books, 2005).

·· CHAPTER FOUR ··

J. Donald Walters, *Education for Life: Preparing Children to Meet the Challenges* (Nevada City, CA: Crystal Clarity, 1997).

·· CHAPTER FIVE ··

Richard Carlson, *Don't Sweat the Small Stuff . . . and It's All Small Stuff* (New York: Hyperion, 1997).

Malcolm Gladwell, *Blink: The Power of Thinking without Thinking* (New York: Little, Brown, 2005).

Francis Hodgson Burnett, *The Secret Garden* (New York: Morrow, 2000).

Lorna Knox, *Scary News: 12 Ways to Raise Joyful Children When the Headlines Are Full of Fear* (Nevada City, CA: Crystal Clarity, 2004).

.... CHAPTER SIX ....

Carla Hannaford, *Awakening the Child Heart* (Captain Cook, HI: Jamilla Nur, 2002).

.... CHAPTER SEVEN ....

Martha Graham,
http://womenshistory.aboutcom/cs/quotes/a/qu_graham_m.htm

.... CHAPTER EIGHT ....

J. Donald Walters, *The Path: One Man's Quest on the Only Path There Is* (Nevada City, CA: Crystal Clarity, 2003).

.... CHAPTER NINE ....

Howard Gardner, "The Intelligences," in *Educational Leadership*, Sept. 1997.

.... CHAPTER TEN ....

Eknath Easwaran, *Original Goodness* (Petaluma, CA: Nilgiri Press, 1989).

.... CHAPTER ELEVEN ....

Mary M. Belknap, *Homo deva* (Berkeley, CA: Lifethread Institute, 2004).

Leonard Pitts, "Taking to the Road to Show His Sons a Higher Path," *The Oregonian*, April 2, 2002.

Stephen G. Post, "It's Good to Be Good," *Science and Theology News*, May 11, 2005. www.stnews.org/Altruism-491.htm.

Lindsey Tanner, "Toddler Study Finds TV Raises Risk of Attention Problems," in *The Oregonian*, April 5, 2004.

Tom Lickona, *Character Matters* (New York: Touchstone, 2004).

Elaine St. James, *Inner Simplicity* (New York: Hyperion, 1995).

Michael Nitai Deranja. *For Goodness' Sake* (Nevada City, CA: Crystal Clarity, 2004).

Carla Hannaford, *Awakening the Child Heart* (Captain Cook, HI: Jamilla Nur, 2002).

Tobin Hart, *The Secret Spiritual World of Children* (Maui, HI: Inner Ocean, 2003).

"The Science of Meditation," *Time*, August 4, 2003.

Contemplative Outreach website, www.centeringprayer.com.

Eknath Easwaran, *Original Goodness* (Petaluma, CA: Nilgiri Press, 1989).

INDEX